Contents

Acknowledgements

Our thanks are due to the assistants in the Borough of Poole for their enthusiasm and dedication. Thanks also to the Literacy and Numeracy Support Service for ideas and inspiration.

We would like to say a big thank you to Margaret Miller for typing the manuscript and to Steven Davis, James Quinnell and Martin Rowson for the cartoons.

Thanks also to Mike, Chris and Jon Halliwell; Paul, Daniel, Ben, Hannah and Elizabeth Fox, for providing personal support systems. And not least to our mothers, Joyce Jones and Phyllis Kreppel who encouraged in us a love of reading.

Glenys Fox,
Principal Educational Psychologist

Marian Halliwell,
Head of Literacy and Numeracy Support Service

Borough of Poole
April 2000

Purpose
The purpose of this book is to enable assistants to work more effectively in supporting children with literacy and/or numeracy difficulties. It is a book which can complement training courses. It is also a useful book for parents supporting their children in learning to read, write, spell or do maths.

Audience
This book is intended as a resource for:
- assistants who support children in the development of their literacy and numeracy skills;
- assistants who come into contact with pupils who have specific difficulties in literacy and numeracy;
- parents who wish to support their child's progress in literacy and numeracy;
- special needs coordinators and teachers who work with assistants;
- training course providers and assistants on courses.

Overview:
There are sections on:
- the current context;
- the literacy strategy;
- the numeracy strategy;
- roles and responsibilities;
- giving support;
- how children learn and what stops them from learning;
- teachers and assistants working together to support literacy and numeracy.

Introduction

The number of Teaching Assistants working in both mainstream and special schools has increased dramatically in recent years. The Government's Green Paper *Excellence for All Children; Meeting Special Educational Needs* (DfEE 1997) recognised the need for assistants to be trained so that their effectiveness in working with teachers and supporting children can be maximised. Another recent Government Green Paper *Teachers Meeting the Challenge of Change* (DfEE 1998b) indicated that there will be an increase in the number of assistants who will provide general support in mainstream schools, not just restricted to children who have special educational needs (SEN). All children need to develop sound literacy and numeracy skills early in their school lives and there are now clear structures in place, the Literacy Hour and the daily maths lesson, to support primary schools in achieving this. There are also plans to give additional help to students in secondary schools who may need it.

There are many assistants in our schools giving support to children who have difficulties in developing literacy and numeracy skills. Many such children attend local mainstream schools but there are also children in special schools who need additional support to improve literacy and numeracy.

The school environment places high value on academic attainment and many subjects require literacy and numeracy skills, so if a child finds it hard to read, write, spell or understand maths then that child is at a disadvantage compared with his or her classmates. Success in these areas is very important both in terms of self-esteem and in coping with the demands of later life.

The Department for Education and Employment (DfEE) recognises the importance of success in these basic skills for all children and government ministers are keen to raise the standards of literacy and numeracy in our schools.

In 1998 the Department introduced the National Literacy Strategy and the Literacy Hour is now an established part of the curriculum in primary schools. The National Numeracy Strategy was introduced in 1999 and all primary schools are now following guidelines to develop the mathematical skills of children.

The work of assistants in supporting these strategies is now recognised and some assistants have followed particular training courses on the subject of literacy and numeracy, in order that they may gain an understanding of how children learn these important basic skills, and how best to work with teachers in order to encourage success.

The teaching of 'the three r's – reading, writing and arithmetic' – has always been a priority, especially for primary teachers, but both the literacy and the numeracy strategies place new emphasis on these skills.

Structured frameworks for use by teachers with graded tasks are provided and careful monitoring of children's progress is made. The aim is that every child should do as well as possible in reading, writing, spelling and numeracy skills, so that in later life they are able to access employment and leisure opportunities. Current statistics show that, at the present time, one in twelve young people leave our schools without any qualifications and one in nine do not go on to work, further education or training, so these strategies have been introduced in order to reduce that number and enhance the life chances of a considerable number of children in our society.

These literacy and numeracy strategies have implications for the work of assistants and their roles are clearly prescribed.

A recent research report from the University of Manchester (1999), *The Management, Role and Training of Learning Support Assistants* describes 'the increasing involvement of assistants in supporting teachers in implementing the National Literacy Strategy, where the role is more clearly defined and the level of prescription results in everyone sharing clear objectives'.

As part of this report, the researchers visited a number of schools to investigate the role of assistants and, in relation to the Literacy Hour, they have this to say:

> A striking feature of the site visits to the primary schools was the role played by assistants in helping to implement the literacy hour. Teaching staff in particular stated that managing the literacy hour with assistants in class to support pupils with special needs had made them look at the role in a much wider and more flexible way. The classroom management with an assistant present had altered in other lessons apart from the literacy hour. A flexibility, which they felt they were obliged to use within the hour, had been transferred to other situations.

This book sets out to provide assistants with an understanding of how children learn to read, write, spell and do maths. It also describes the barriers to learning and the role of the assistant in removing some of those barriers. The conditions necessary for optimum learning to take place are discussed. The book aims to give practical advice so that assistants can be as effective as possible in supporting children in learning these important skills.

Where do I start?

Chapter 1

Roles and responsibilities

In your work as an assistant you will be working as part of the learning support team in the school. The head teacher is responsible for all the teaching and learning which takes place in the school but delegates some of this responsibility to class teachers and the special needs coordinator (SENCO). Support arrangements vary from school to school. In large secondary schools, assistants normally are managed by the SENCO who explains roles and responsibilities in respect of particular children or groups of children. In a primary school, or special school, the SENCO may have less of a role in managing your direct work. If you work closely with one particular class teacher then he or she is likely to play a major part in guiding your day-to-day work.

Whether it is the SENCO or the class teacher who works most closely with you, it is important that they ensure that:

- you are clear about your responsibilities in the classroom;
- you have time to discuss your role in supporting individual education plans for children;
- you are given clear and realistic requests;
- you understand the learning implications for the pupils who find literacy and numeracy difficult;
- you are encouraged and supported in your work.

Who will explain my responsibilities?

In general terms, your role in giving support is discussed in Chapter 2. In supporting pupils who have difficulty in developing literacy or numeracy skills, the teacher may ask you to work in one of four ways:

- working with the pupil in the classroom;
- working with a small group;
- working individually with the pupil;
- developing or choosing resources.

What will I be asked to do?

In all these ways of working, your main purpose is to encourage the child to work independently, without support from you if at all possible. Some pupils become too dependent on assistants who work with them and learn to feel helpless when the assistant is not there.

Working with the pupil in the classroom

Enabling a pupil to be a part of the whole class is an important role for an assistant to play. Most children want to belong to their class group so if support can be given within the classroom then this ideally is the way it should be given. Children have quite strong views about this issue and it is important to get their ideas about what works best for them. Some are very happy to have an assistant close by to support the work they are doing. Others, particularly older children and teenagers, hate the idea of having a 'minder', so for these pupils, support may best be given outside the main class group. The pressure to conform and be like everyone else becomes very strong in adolescence and pupils fear that they may be ridiculed if others think they cannot read or write well.

Be sensitive to the wishes of the pupil and talk with the teacher about the best location for support to be given. There is an increasing recognition that all children need to be included in mainstream classes as much as possible so this must always be the first location to consider support arrangements. Only if conditions in the mainstream class cannot be made compatible with effective learning for the child, should alternatives be considered.

Working with a small group

You may be asked to work with a small group, either as part of the Literacy Hour or as a specific activity appropriate for a small group of pupils at another point in the school day.

When a small number of children sit round a table they naturally form a social group. Ideally this leads to cooperation and joint learning, but if handled badly it can cause conflict and negative comparisons. So whenever you have a small group together it is important to set down expectations for behaviour before you work with them on the task. Depending on the age of the pupils you may have to demonstrate and teach the behaviours you need from the group in order for them to settle to the task. Some examples might be:

- follow directions first time;
- when one person speaks we all listen;
- sit on your chair properly;
- keep noise level low.

When you are working with a small group it is important to 'keep all the plates spinning'. This means having all the pupils engaged in doing the task for as much time as possible. You will need to give each child attention at intervals during the activity and not spend too much time with one child or the others may get restless. It is therefore essential to ensure that each pupil knows what they have to do at the start of the activity and has all the equipment necessary.

Many children who have poor literacy skills also have poor memories so it will be helpful to give frequent reminders of what the activity involves.

Working individually with the pupil

Some pupils find it hard to concentrate in the main classroom and become easily distracted by noise and movement. Others, as mentioned already, hate to be picked out as different by having an assistant working alongside. For these pupils, it is sometimes more effective to locate the assistance outside the classroom where quieter conditions may enable more effective working and the pupil is not distracted by others. When you work in a one-to-one relationship with a pupil it can be quite demanding and you will need clear directions from the class teacher about what you should be doing. For this work to be successful you need to establish a positive relationship, so it will be helpful to find out some of the child's interests so you can have conversations about these topics and encourage him or her to talk. Try to listen for points which reflect the child's skill in some way and comment on these points, e.g. 'You are a very good granddaughter, helping your gran like that'. 'What a lot you know about Manchester United, I am really impressed by all the facts you tell me.' This sets a 'can do' tone for the session and is particularly important for children whose self-esteem is poor because they feel they cannot read, write or do number work.

As mentioned above, in-class support is usually preferable to isolated activities but there are some tasks which may be better done away from the class group (but *only* when the pupil cannot concentrate within the classroom setting and conditions cannot be changed).

Such individual tasks may be:

- following specific programmes of work;
- accessing particular reading/spelling programs on the computer
- reading/sharing a book;
- finishing off a piece of work which is different from that in the classroom.

Working away from the class group should be minimised as far as possible both for one-to-one and small group work.

Developing or choosing resources

This may or may not be an appropriate thing for you to do, much depends on the particular child or children you are working with and how the teacher sees your role. However, it is a useful role for assistants to play, particularly if you are supporting pupils who have literacy or numeracy difficulties. As you become familiar with the schemes of work the class is following and of the particular abilities of the pupils you are working with, you will be aware of what they can and cannot do.

It is therefore very helpful if you can look in advance at what might be required, what worksheets will be used, etc., and take some time to modify these under the teacher's guidance so that the child is not presented with a task they have no chance of understanding because it is at too high a level for them or there is too much information on the sheet.

Modifying tasks and materials to be understood at a number of different levels is called differentiation and if you can do this with the end result that the pupil is successful in the task, then this is a valuable contribution you can make.

If you are working with younger children on developing language activities or number skills you may find it is better to invent your own games for children to play. Many assistants, as part of training courses, have developed some innovative, bright and attractive resources, activities or games to inspire the children and young people with whom they work. There are a great many resources and activities commercially produced to support language, literacy and numeracy (some of which are referred to in later chapters of this book). You will benefit from knowing what is available in the school resources cupboard so that you can choose specific activities to match the needs of the pupils you work with. Games and visual aids can be of enormous benefit, particularly if they make learning more fun.

What specific tasks will I be doing?

In supporting children who have literacy or numeracy difficulties there are particular activities which you may be asked to support. Advice on how to do this follows later in this book but the following list is a guide to what you may be asked to do as part of your role together with some examples of what this might involve:

- helping pupils to have equipment ready and be able to use it;
- helping the pupil to understand the task;
- helping the pupil to understand the sequence needed to complete the task;
- helping the pupil in knowing where to find relevant information;
- checking the work pupils produce and helping them to correct their own mistakes;
- giving the pupil strategies to help in remembering information;
- guiding computer-assisted learning programs;
- sharing a book/hearing a child read;
- preparing audio tapes, encouraging the use of a dictaphone and acting as scribe;
- encouraging the use of a word processor;
- reading textbook sections or questions and testing the pupil's understanding;
- helping to catch up with missed work;
- observation of how a pupil works or manages a particular task.

Helping pupils to have equipment ready and be able to use it

Children who have literacy difficulties are often disorganised in their thinking so it will help if you can encourage the child you are working with to have equipment ready for the lesson. A pencil case kept in a usual place with a sharpened pencil and working pens, rubbers, etc., can avoid the need for time-wasting at the start of an activity. (Some children have perfected his particular time-wasting activity as a strategy for avoiding work they find hard!)

Some children benefit from using a handheld spellchecker so you will need to check whether they understand how to use it for maximum benefit.

Helping the pupil to understand the task

Children with literacy difficulties often have very poor short-term memories for verbal instructions given by the teacher. You can help by using a technique called 'perception checking' which simply means that you prime the child to listen to the instructions, then following the instructions, you say to the child 'Now tell me what the teacher just said'. If the child knows that you are going to be checking his or her listening, then he or she is more likely to make an effort to listen and understand. However, don't expect the child to remember long instructions as there may be genuine difficulties in doing this. Practising this skill is, however, very important.

Helping the pupil to understand the sequence needed to complete the task

When instructions are given by the teacher, most pupils are aware of the sequence of actions needed to get to the end of the task, e.g. start with headings, look up information, make notes, do diagrams, etc.

Children who have literacy difficulties often find it difficult to sequence ideas in their minds so it is helpful if you can 'map out' the sequence needed at the start of the task to aid the child in understanding what should be done first, second, etc., and encourage the child to do this for themselves. 'Sam, what is the first thing you're going to have to do here...and then what...?' and so on.

Helping the pupil in knowing where to find relevant information

As we have mentioned, disorganisation is often a characteristic of children who have literacy difficulties. Your role might be to help them in organising information and accessing what is needed to complete a task successfully. If the class is doing particular topic work it may be helpful to record the common words used as part of that topic as a list inside the child's folder.

If words have to be looked up in a dictionary or topics in an encyclopaedia, do recognise that some children cannot remember the alphabet sequence so will have difficulties knowing where to find the information. Some children have 'word finding' difficulties, that is they cannot say the word they want to say because they cannot 'find' it in their memory. In these cases you may need to suggest alternatives and allow the pupil to identify the right one.

Checking the work pupils produce and helping them to correct their own mistakes

It is important that you encourage children to work without leaning on you too much for support, they should not feel inhibited from doing a task because they think they might 'get it wrong'. If you are asked to look at a piece of work which has a lot of mistakes, do try and make some positive comments about it before encouraging the child to correct their mistakes. For example, 'Sophie, I like the way you have set this work out and the drawing is good, now let's look at this first sentence, can you see a word which has the wrong spelling, one that you can put right?'

Giving the pupil strategies to help in remembering information

For the majority of pupils, giving verbal instructions is enough for them to understand and remember what to do in order to complete the task. Pupils who have literacy difficulties frequently need more than just verbal instructions to enable them to be successful. They need what is called a 'multi-sensory' approach, which means using more than just their sense of hearing to take in and retain information. So visual prompts and kinaesthetic (movement) prompts can also aid children in remembering information, e.g. having a luggage label attached to their schoolbag which lists the activities and equipment needed for the day; for children who confuse the letters 'b' and 'd' helping them to visualise the word 'bed' as a bed with the 'ends tucked in'.

The use of mnemonics – memory prompts using verse or unusual sentences based on a sequence can be helpful – (e.g. 'Thirty days hath September' etc., for remembering the numbers of days in each month).

Guiding computer-assisted learning programs

There are now many IT programs available to support the development of literacy and numeracy and they have made a great contribution to supporting development. Children like these programs as they are often bright and attractive.

Additionally, they are non-judgemental so if a child gets something wrong there is no disapproval but just a 'try again' message. Each will have its particular instructions. It is really important that you familiarise yourself with using these programs (ask to be shown!) so that you can include this resource as a part of your work in supporting literacy and numeracy. But do ensure it is at the right level!

Sharing a book/hearing a child read

For a child who can read, listening to fluent reading and helping with the occasional mistake is an easy job. However, for a child who finds reading difficult, it is a complex and quite sophisticated skill which requires an understanding of what is preventing the child from reading well in the first place. This is discussed further in Chapter 4 but guidance from the teacher or SENCO in how best to do this is essential if you are to make this activity into a positive experience for the child.

It's your turn now

Preparing audiotapes, encouraging the use of a dictaphone and acting as scribe

As the pupil may not be able to write down easily the information they know about a particular topic, you can encourage them to use a dictaphone to record their knowledge or to write an essay. You can then lend support by transcribing the information and encouraging the pupil to copy what you have written, which is, in fact, their contribution.

If their writing is slow and laborious then it is not helpful to expect them to write out a long piece. Be realistic in your expectations. Practise the key words used and work on setting out a piece of work which is achievable.

You may also assist the pupil by making notes of key words while the teacher is talking or while a TV programme is being watched. Recording particular topic words and keeping them to hand is particularly useful as is a list of commonly used words in writing.

Encouraging the use of a word processor

Information technology (IT) is of enormous benefit in helping children and young people to set their work out neatly and reduce spelling mistakes by using the 'spellcheck' facility.

Pupils gain confidence in doing this and start to think of themselves as capable of producing legible and correct pieces of work. If there is a facility at the school you work at to support the development of typing skills, then it will be well worth supporting the pupil to learn these skills.

Reading textbook sections or questions and testing the pupil's understanding

If the pupil you are working with is not able to read well, then it will often be helpful for you to read passages to them or questions which have been set. You might find it useful to question the pupil as you go along to ensure he or she is listening and understanding.

Helping to catch up with missed work

Sometimes you may be asked to help the pupil complete a piece of work which he or she has been slow to do in class. This can sometimes be unmotivating so you will need all your powers of encouragement to do this. Realistic expectations are crucial to success and no task should be so difficult that it drags on and on! Discuss this with the class teacher if it is becoming too much of a chore.

Observation of how a pupil works or manages a particular task

In your work with children or young people, you can sometimes learn a lot by stepping back from the situation and observing carefully how the pupil works. You will become aware of the external factors which influence working, e.g. noise level, who is sitting near the pupil, whether he or she can settle to work and the role of the teacher in making instructions clear to everyone. In doing this you might see that the pupil would do better if particular conditions were changed, e.g. sitting the child next to good role models may encourage working and cooperative peers can give the pupil some of the guidance and support he or she needs.

In observing a pupil you may become aware of how much independent work he or she is capable of without adult support or you may recognise non-human resources which can aid the child in a particular task, e.g. spelling lists or 'model' sums.

In fulfilling your roles and responsibilities it is important for you to take a step back periodically and ask yourself, 'Is what I am doing, working?'

If the answer is 'yes' then pat yourself on the back, share this with the teacher and keep up the good work!

If the answer is 'no' then you need to think about what is preventing progress. You may find that talking with the teacher or SENCO will enable you to make changes. Chapter 3, on how children learn, might also give you some ideas about what may be blocking the learning process.

How will I know that I am doing the job right?

How will I be supported through training?

The DfEE have planned training programmes for assistants. The guidance has this to say:

Proposals for literacy

The teaching assistants' training programme for literacy is designed to induct new assistants into literacy and provide strategies that they can use alongside teachers to raise pupil attainment. The training programme will draw on the experience of the National Literacy Strategy in training assistants to support the literacy development of identified groups of pupils across the primary age range.

The aims of the programme are as follows:

- to introduce teaching assistants to the Early Learning Goals and the content of the English National Curriculum and the National Literacy Strategy;

- to develop a range of strategies to enable new teaching assistants to work flexibly and support the literacy development of pupils across the age range;
- to introduce teaching assistants to the planning process;
- to help teaching assistants deploy a variety of resources appropriate to the age range they are supporting;
- to enable teaching assistants to assist in the assessment and recording of pupil progress;
- to introduce teaching assistants to further professional development, e.g. specialist teacher assistant (STA) training and programmes designed to support specific groups of pupils, e.g. Additional Literacy Strategy (ALS).

Proposals for mathematics

The programme is designed to enable new assistants to work alongside teachers throughout the primary age range to raise levels of pupil attainment in mathematics.

The programme will introduce participants to:
- the principal characteristics of the National Numeracy Strategy and *The Framework for Teaching Mathematics* (DfEE 1999b);
- the three-part daily mathematics lesson and the role of the teaching assistant in each part;
- the approach to mental calculations;
- working with children; helping pupils who find mathematics difficult to catch up;
- working in the reception class;
- appropriate mathematical activities and resources to support and consolidate learning.

Chapter 2

Giving support

The principles of giving support to any child are the same whatever the learning difficulty might be. So for supporting children who find reading, writing or number work difficult, the following general advice applies. This advice is about how you make the learning environment as effective as possible.

When teaching assistants are asked to define their supporting role, their responses fall into three main categories:

* supporting the pupil;
* supporting the teacher;
* supporting the school.

Assistants identify the following aspects of their supportive role with pupils:

* promoting independence;
* inspiring confidence and trust;
* valuing the child;
* fostering peer group acceptance;
* encouraging and giving rewards;
* developing listening skills;
* enabling the child;
* knowing the background;
* finding out about the learning support needs;
* keeping confidences;
* being 'in tune' with the child's physical needs.

How can I support the pupil?

Promoting independence

This is a key concept in considering your role. You are there to give a high level of support initially, but as time goes on, you must seek to encourage the pupil to attempt new tasks without your support. It is common for assistants to feel that they must always be 'one step ahead', but, in fact, the idea of being 'one step behind' is much more helpful in promoting the independence of the pupil. If you are always foreseeing pitfalls and removing them from the path of the pupil, then he or she will never learn strategies for coping in the real world.

There will, however, be times when you will have to act in order to pre-empt serious situations – common sense is a necessary quality!

Some assistants feel that if they are employed to work with one particular pupil, then it is appropriate to 'stick like glue' to that pupil. Though there are times when the child will need individual support, it will often be appropriate to help the pupil within a small group or even to spend time standing back and observing the behaviour of the pupil in classroom situations. You may be surprised at how much he or she is capable of. You will be doing the child no favours if you encourage dependence on you. In fact, you should be aiming to be so effective in promoting the independence of the pupil that you work yourself out of a job!

Inspiring confidence and trust

Often it is the case that pupils with SEN are lacking in confidence. Children become aware of failure very quickly and they lose confidence when they see their classmates making progress while they struggle.

Pupils who have had difficult social histories may feel that they have been 'let down' by the important adults in their lives and feel it is hard to trust someone to be consistent, fair and encouraging. A pupil with a low opinion of himself or herself, for whatever reason, is going to begin to expect to fail. It is, therefore, vital that you take every opportunity to point out what the pupil is good at and to lead them to expect that they can succeed. Think out ways of providing frequent opportunities for real success. It may take time but if you have a consistent, positive and fair attitude towards the child, he or she will learn to develop confidence and to trust you.

Valuing the child

No child can learn effectively when they are not feeling valued. It is a key role of a teaching assistant to value the child. Any child who is thought of as 'different' from other pupils may encounter negative attitudes particularly if the disability is obvious. Surviving childhood teasing is often dependent on self-esteem, so it is very important that the child feels secure and highly regarded by the important people in his or her life and you are one of them.

Wow!

Fostering peer group acceptance

It is part of your role to encourage the other pupils to value the child. This entails drawing attention to those skills the child is good at, or to some particular achievement of the child. It may also involve valuing the contributions of the child, e.g. making the child group leader in appropriate activities.

Some children need help to improve social skills, i.e. the way they relate to others. If the child you work with has poor social skills then you can help him or her by practising appropriate responses – first in play-acting then in real situations. For younger children it might be helpful to act out a well-known fairy tale, e.g. Billy Goats Gruff, with each child being able to take on different roles. This can help children explore feelings and relationships – the troll seen as a 'bully' and the little billy goat Gruff seen as the 'victim'. This sort of activity can lead on to discussions about feelings and rights and wrongs. For older pupils, discussing real situations and then role-playing to consider the best outcomes can be extremely helpful.

Encouraging and giving rewards

Giving the pupil encouragement and praise is a very important part of your role and will contribute in a large part to the development of self-esteem and confidence. Liberal amounts of praise must be given.

Meaningful praise means telling the pupil why you are pleased with him or her, e.g. it is better to say 'Gemma, I like the way you have used colour in this picture', rather than 'That's a good picture', or 'Tom, you listened to the story well today', rather than just 'Good boy'.

All children respond to rewards if the rewards are motivating and achievable. It will help you in your work with the pupil if you can work out, early on in your relationship, something tangible. Here are some ideas you might suggest to the child as incentives, but remember to ask the child first what they would like as a reward once they have achieved what you have negotiated.

Primary age pupils

- extra 'choosing time', when he or she can choose an activity;
- extra time on the computer;
- a favourite game;
- a bubble-blowing session;
- making biscuits, cakes or sweets;
- stickers to wear and keep;
- decorating plain biscuits with icing and 'sprinkles';
- doing an 'important' job for the class teacher or head teacher;
- music while you work;
- letter or certificate sent home to parents.

Secondary age pupils

- extra time on the computer;
- letter or certificate sent home to parents;
- position of responsibility;
- a special interest project;
- free ticket to school disco.

It is important to ensure that the reward is achievable over a short period of time to start with, so that success is encouraged. For younger children particularly, the reward needs to be earned within one day so that it is immediate. Other children may be able to work towards a reward at the end of two or three days, or at the end of a week. Again, you will need to negotiate this with the class teacher so that there is consistency in your approach.

Developing listening skills

When you start work with a pupil, it is tempting to do a lot of the talking and to expect that the pupil has taken in what you have said. Remember that effective communication is a two-way process and that some children need time to get their thoughts together and to express themselves. Some are only able to understand short bits of information at a time. You may need to check that the pupil has understood by asking him or her to repeat back to you the information you have given or that the teacher has given to the class. This simple technique is called 'perception checking' and is an extremely valuable skill to practise and use regularly.

Pupils with emotional difficulties can be helped enormously by someone providing a 'listening ear'. This means that when the pupil is talking, you give him or her your full attention and are able to make encouraging gestures such as nodding and smiling. Non-verbal 'messages' from you to the child are, in fact, more important than the words you use.

You can learn to encourage pupils to talk by choosing the right phrases. This is called Active Listening. Brenda Mallon, in her book *An Introduction to Counselling Skills for Special Educational Needs*, gives the following examples, (Table 2.1):

Types	Purpose	Examples
Warmth, Support	To help the pupil	'I'd like to help you; are you able to tell me about what is the matter?'
Clarification	To get the complete 'story' from the pupil	'Can you tell me more about it?' 'Do you mean...?'
Restatement	To check our meaning is the same as the pupil's	'From what you are saying, I understand that...'
Encouragement	To encourage the pupil	'I realise this is difficult for you but you are doing really well'
Reflective	To act as a mirror so the pupil can see what is being communicated	'You feel that...' 'It was very hard for you to accept...'
	To help pupils evaluate their feelings	'You felt angry and upset when...'
	To show you understand the feelings behind the words	'I can see you are feeling upset...'
Summarising	To bring together the points raised	'These are the main things you have told me...' 'As I see it, your main worry seems to be...'

Table 2.1 Listening skills

If you are able to use some of these skills then you will be well on the way to being a good listener and, more than that, you will help the pupil to work through whatever is causing worry or concern.

Enabling the child

The pupil who needs learning support often feels unable to attempt tasks which other pupils have no problem with. Your role is not to do the task for the pupil, but to enable the pupil to do that task for himself or herself by providing the necessary 'tools for the job'. This may mean:

- explaining the task clearly when the pupil has not understood (if the problem persists, see the teacher);
- making sure the pupil knows what equipment is necessary, where it is kept and how to use it;
- helping the pupil to organise his or her thoughts and consider how to set out the work;
- encouraging the pupil to arrive at the lesson on time and with the correct equipment;
- giving the pupil strategies to use to help him or her remember information, e.g. writing lists, keeping a diary;
- working with small groups to encourage sharing and cooperation.

Your role is not to do the task for the pupil!

You may need to adapt the worksheet provided by the teacher so that the pupil can understand and do the task. Making a task simpler in this way is called differentiation and it is done so that the child is more likely to understand and learn.

Knowing the background

You will understand the pupil's difficulties better if you know something about the pupil's home life and the way he or she spends time out of school.

It will help you in establishing a relationship if you find out early on who the other family members are, whether the pupil has any pets and what hobbies or special interests he or she has. You may find it valuable, particularly with younger children, to keep a scrapbook entitled 'All About Me', into which you can put photographs and snippets of written information about what happens in the life of the child. The child will feel valued when you show interest in the things which are meaningful to him or her.

For the older child this can also be a useful activity. Writing an autobiography, 'My Life Story', can be particularly helpful to pupils who have emotional difficulties and low self-esteem.

Finding out about the learning support needs

It is the responsibility of the class teacher or the SENCO in the school to ensure that you know what you need to know about the child's particular needs, in order to do the job. If you feel you don't know, do ask. There is likely to be a register of children at different stages of the Code of Practice in the school together with Individual Education Plans (IEPs).

There is a network of services external to the school, e.g. speech therapists, physiotherapists, teacher advisers, educational psychologists and child psychiatrists who can be approached, together with your class teacher, should you want to find out more information.

There are also many charitable organisations which offer information about a wide range of disabilities, e.g. SCOPE (formerly the Spastics Society) and the Royal National Institute for the Blind.

The information contained in the child's school records will give you some background knowledge. You will need to check with the head teacher whether you can have access to this information.

Keeping confidences

This follows on well from the last point. When you work closely with a child there are bound to be times when you hear or see information, e.g. about the child's home life, which must be kept confidential. This does not apply, however, to disclosure of child abuse, which is information you have a duty to share with the head teacher.

In the course of your job, you may find people confiding in you. While you can discuss information with other professionals concerned, remember that the information you come across in the course of your job is not for discussion or comment with outsiders.

Being 'in tune' with the child's physical needs

This refers to the physical well-being of the child. There are occasions when a child comes to school feeling tired, hungry or just not well. This is particularly the case with pupils who have physical disabilities and who may have had disturbed sleep.

Show an interest in the child's interests

Children from non-nurturing homes are also at risk. When working with such children, the session is not always likely to be an academic success.

Don't feel you have failed if nothing is achieved on paper sometimes – quite often, showing a genuine interest in the child and lending a sympathetic ear goes a long way towards compensating for what may be lacking in the child's background. Be aware of any moodiness or lethargy and make allowances for it. Imagine how you feel yourself when you are tired or run-down, and treat the child with gentleness and sensitivity.

When working with secondary age pupils you may need to be alert to signs of drug taking and be prepared to report back to the SENCO if you are concerned.

Assistants identified the following aspects of their supportive role with respect to the class teacher:

- working in partnership;
- providing feedback about how the pupil manages the work given;
- helping in setting targets, monitoring and evaluating Individual Education Plans;
- recording information;
- maintaining a sense of humour.

How can I support the teacher?

Working in partnership

Working in any partnership implies *communication*. In order to work well with a class teacher you must feel able to ask questions, clarify expectations and get feedback on your work with the pupil. It is a two-way process and obviously much depends on the personality and organisational skills of the teacher, on whom you are dependent for direction and guidance.

However, if you are to work effectively it is vital that you meet regularly for information exchange, joint planning and evaluation. In a primary school it need only be for a short time each day or each week but it is in the best interests of the pupils that you do this. In a secondary school this is more difficult as you may be supporting the pupil in up to ten curriculum areas.

You may find it more practical to have one longer planning session per month. Planning does take some time commitment by the class teacher but you will be better able to support him or her if you are both clear about what you are both doing. To quote from the Audit Commission/HMI handbook (1992): 'Where extra help is provided, planning and communication are the keys to improving its impact'.

This document also stresses the need for the supporting adult to 'be aware of the class teacher's objectives for a piece of work so that he or she can then focus on what the child is to master, and consider alternative means of reaching the same goal'.

Working in partnership can be a problem, particularly for assistants in secondary schools who will have to work with a number of different teachers. Some staff may have subject specialisms and it may be sometimes necessary for you to ensure that a member of staff understands the way in which you can assist a pupil in a given situation and the limitations of that pupil.

A small minority of teachers feel threatened by the presence of another adult in the classroom. If you feel uncomfortable about any situation it may help to discuss your concerns with the SENCO and the teacher concerned. But do remember that your main role is not to give 'marks out of ten' for the quality of any lesson or any teaching style, but to act in the best interests of the pupils whom you are employed to support and enable them to make the best of any teaching situation.

Providing feedback about the pupil

In working closely with a particular pupil or group of pupils, it is likely that you will be more sensitive to their needs and reactions in any given situation than is the class teacher, who takes a wider view. You will be able, therefore, to provide information to the teacher about how well the pupil is coping with the demands made on him or her. This may involve written feedback or record keeping.

If a task given to the pupil is too difficult, don't feel you must persevere with it to the bitter end but feed back to the teacher that this is the case and either get the teacher to modify the task or agree that you yourself can do this. Teaching assistants are often wonderfully creative given the opportunity, so feel confident in making suggestions and modifications as you feel necessary. The majority of teachers will be only too pleased to hear your ideas and take them on board if possible.

In addition to feedback about how the pupil is coping with school work you will also be able to provide information about the general well-being of the pupil and about situations out of school or in the playground which may be affecting the pupil's performance in class.

Helping in setting targets, monitoring and evaluating programmes

In an ideal situation, when you are meeting regularly with the class teacher or SENCO, you will be able to make a contribution to the planning of IEPs. It is the responsibility of the class teacher and possibly the SENCO to do this for each pupil with special needs, as they might be deciding exactly what is the next step for the pupil. You will be able to contribute ideas about how this might be done, bearing in mind the temperament of the pupil.

It is also extremely valuable to *evaluate* what you are doing with the pupil. This means 'taking a step back' periodically, say every half term, or even more frequently, and asking yourself just how effective your work with the pupil has been and whether the targets or goals set have been achieved. If not, or only partially, it would be worth discussing alternative approaches with the class teacher in order to see if this makes a difference. But do remember that many children who need learning support often learn only slowly and so realistic expectations are clearly needed.

Recording information

As part of your work in supporting the teacher, it is essential that you record what you do in the course of your work with the pupils. The class teacher or SENCO will be able to advise you about the sort of records you should keep and the format this should take. The information you will be asked to record will depend on the particular needs of the pupil.

For instance, you may be asked to record details about the language the child uses or about how many times he or she shows aggressive behaviour. Whatever the record is, it should contain useful information to help in planning future work rather than just a diary of events. So it might, therefore, be useful to record the date, the activity and the materials used, bearing in mind why you are doing the task. It would then be useful to record an evaluative comment about how well the pupil succeeded in the task. In any record, it is very important to record successes as well as difficulties. Feeding back success to the teacher will improve the motivation of the child.

Consider:

- Has the pupil learned? If not, why not? (task too hard, wrong time of day, too many distractions, unmotivating materials, etc.);
- How might this be done better next time? (Discuss with teacher).

Maintaining a sense of humour

When a teacher has a pupil or pupils with special needs in his or her class it can sometimes become hard work as progress is often slow and the level of attention demanded by these pupils is often high. For the health and sanity of the teacher, the pupil and yourself it is a good thing to smile and joke about situations which invite it. Do not allow situations to become too 'heavy' – having a sense of optimism and good humour can help the teacher and the pupils enormously.

Avoid using sarcasm as this can be damaging to the self-esteem of the pupil. Mutual support of teacher and teaching assistant can be of tremendous benefit.

Suggestion to enhance mutual support

Take some time to sit down with the teacher(s) you work with and do the following exercise:

I am a teaching assistant. How can I best support the teacher?

I am a teacher. How can I best support the teaching assistant?

How can I support the school?

Assistants identify the following aspects of their supportive role within the school:

- working as part of the learning support 'team';
- working with parents;
- contributing to reviews;
- knowing the school procedures;
- attending relevant in-service training or staff meetings;
- using particular personal strengths.

Working as part of the learning support 'team'

Within the school this team will consist of the class teacher(s), the teaching assistants and the SENCO, who has a general overview of all pupils in the school who need learning support. In secondary schools the Year head and class tutor may also have a role. The head teacher has overall responsibility for you and may take an active interest, but usually the role of supervision is delegated to the SENCO or class teacher.

There are other professionals whose workbase is outside the school but who come into school regularly to give advice about pupils with SEN and are therefore part of a wider support network. These include educational psychologists, physiotherapists, occupational therapists, speech and language therapists and advisory teachers. These people will be pleased to discuss with you any relevant issues related to your work.

In an ideal situation, you will feel valued and supported if colleagues in the school see you as part of a team.

Giving you the opportunity to be involved in planning and decision-making will encourage your own ideas and creativity and you will feel more positive about your role in the school. This depends largely on the attitudes of other members of staff, some of whom may find partnership-working too threatening and are thus unable to treat you as having a different but equal contribution to make.

More usually, however, it is because staff are too busy to step back from their daily work and plan ahead with you. Too often, assistants are placed in a 'reactive' role – responding to whatever comes up at the time without any planning, rather than a 'proactive' role – taking time to plan intervention in advance.

In order to make the best use of your time, a teamwork approach is vital. Very few teachers would disagree with this. If you feel you are a 'reactive' assistant then discuss with the class teacher and/or SENCO any ideas you might have about improving how your time is used and how you feel the need to be part of a team.

The parents or home carers of the pupils concerned also play a part in this teamwork approach. It is important that they are made aware of the programmes and plans which are being made for their children so that they can be encouraged to support the work of the school at home in whatever way is appropriate. The most important adults in a child's life are the parents and their influence on the child is enormous. It is important that they understand the implications of any difficulty and are helped to be positive in their attitudes and expectations.

Working with parents or carers

Your job may bring you into frequent contact with the child's parents or carers, particularly if the child has physical disabilities. In some cases an important part of your role may be to develop a positive relationship with the parents and to foster links between home and school, working in partnership with the class teacher. At times, it may be necessary to provide a 'listening ear' in order to support the parents and to understand what is going on in the child's home life.

It is necessary to keep a safe distance emotionally when this happens and to beware of getting embroiled in complex family dynamics. It is also necessary to keep confidences which may be shared. The class teacher should be aware of relevant issues and should be able to intervene should things become too 'heavy'. Sometimes it is very hard for parents to accept that their child has a special need. You may have a part to play in helping them to come to terms with this and to be realistic. Valuing what a child is good at and pointing out progress may be part of your role in such a situation.

Contributing to reviews

Every pupil who has a Statement of Special Educational Needs must have a review of their special educational needs, at least annually. This includes a meeting when all concerned with the pupil, both inside the school and outside, can come together, discuss recent reports, inform each other about progress and make plans for meeting the pupil's needs in the future. Pupils without statements may also have internal review meetings.

If you have had close contact with the pupil, you may be asked to give a short verbal or written report at the meeting and if you have kept records they will prove useful in giving your report.

Do remember that there will always be people within the school who will help you to do this and opportunities for you to discuss your contribution before the meeting.

Occasionally there will be case conferences about children with whom you are involved. Such meetings normally follow a pupil's exclusion from school or some concern voiced by the health department or social services.

Again, you may be asked to give your perspective about the pupil's needs. On rare occasions, you could be asked to give your views on a child's needs and progress for court hearings. Your teacher colleagues will support you in doing this. It is important that you give your views in line with the school views about the child's needs, following preparation and discussion of the issues.

'Ahem! Friends, parents and countrymen...'

Knowing the school procedures

You will be able to support the school effectively if you make sure you know about school policies and procedures, e.g. accidents, discipline, bullying, out-of-school visits, child protection, etc. Ask the head teacher what procedures you need to know of if you are unsure.

There will also be ongoing procedural changes. It is unlikely that you will attend all staff meetings (which are normally held outside the LSA contracted hours) so in order to be aware of week-by-week changes, you need to refer to a member of staff, probably the SENCO, who should make you aware of changes, particularly if they affect you. Again, *communication* is the key factor.

'Sorry, did no-one tell you the trip's been postponed until next week?'

Attending relevant in-service training or staff meetings

When opportunities arise to further your knowledge about learning support or to be involved in meetings about whole-school initiatives, then do try to attend. Ideally, this time should come from within your school hours – in reality many assistants choose to work additional hours in order that their pupils do not miss out. This need for training is now being recognised, and provided for in many areas.

Using particular personal strengths

The whole class and maybe the school can benefit if you are prepared to share any particular talent you might have. It could be that you are a good singer or can play an instrument well. Perhaps you have artistic or dramatic talent or maybe your culinary or DIY skills are renowned. Don't hide your light under a bushel – be willing to contribute. And don't underestimate the parenting skills you may have – the vast majority of assistants are parents themselves so can often provide insights about what might be appropriate to solve common childhood problems.

What makes an effective teaching assistant?

The following qualities were described by a group of teaching assistants:

- patience;
- care;
- sense of fairness;
- consistency;
- sensitivity;
- ability to learn from mistakes;
- flexibility;
- versatility;
- positive attitudes;
- friendliness;
- being hard to shock;
- sense of humour;
- enthusiasm.

Most assistants possess many of these qualities and become aware of areas which need to be worked on.

'Saint or superwoman? – or both!'

Chapter 3

How children learn

Learning is essential to our survival! If you think of a newborn baby, it has needs for food, warmth and sleep. Babies are pretty good at letting us know when they need something – determining what *exactly* they need can sometimes be difficult! However, the baby quickly learns how to get attention in order to have needs met. As the baby grows, he or she will start exploring the environment and through daily experiences will learn about how to survive and enjoy the surrounding world. Children are naturally curious and will quickly learn what to do in order to have good experiences rather than bad. Touching a hot pan will result in a hasty recoil and a learning experience which says beware of pans! Finding that it is fun to knock a tower of bricks down encourages the child to build.

The following principles, put together by Hampshire Inspection and Advisory Support Service (1992) are fundamental statements about learning and are true for all children.

Ways in which children learn

- Children learn primarily through practical first-hand experiences.
- Children learn through all their senses (with the rare exception of children who have severe sensory impairment).
- Children make sense of new experiences by relating them to previous learning.
- Children develop their understanding through talking.
- Children have preferred learning styles and learn at different rates.
- Children may move across subject boundaries as they learn.
- Children learn best when they can make sense of what they do through involvement in planning and reflection.
- Children learn through purposeful repetition, practice and reinforcement.
- Children learn best when there is care, tolerance, security, praise and high expectations, associated with clear learning goals.

Let's look at what these principles mean for the development of literacy and numeracy skills.

Children learn primarily through practical first-hand experiences

Young children find opportunities to play and through play they begin to recognise objects and how they work. Manipulating sand, playing with water, sorting stones or shells and playing with commercially produced toys enables the child to develop basic concepts. Usually this starts with ideas of object permanence at around eight months when young children will look for an object that is covered up, getting the idea of objects being there even though not seen. Words such as 'all gone' start to have meaning. Basic ideas of colour and shape are learned and concepts such as up/down, in/out, big/little are among the first to develop in children. If adults around them provide the language to support and guide play and to describe what the child is doing then this helps children to learn at a faster rate. This use of language is very important in enabling the child to learn, because effective understanding and use of language are crucial to the later development of both literacy and numeracy.

There are important early concepts which support children's understanding of number.

Ideas of same and different, more and less, bigger and smaller are basic concepts which help our understanding of number.

The skill of classification, i.e. sorting into groups those items with similar characteristics, is an important skill in the development of both literacy and numeracy.

So we can see how practical first-hand experiences enable learning but this is not just at an early stage. It is always helpful to use equipment when introducing new ideas to older children. Many of them lose the need for these props to learning as they become more able to use written words and numbers, but for children who find it difficult then the use of practical toys, apparatus and equipment will aid understanding.

Children learn through all their senses

We have five senses, sight, hearing, touch, smell and taste. We have already seen how young children use touch, sight and hearing to develop new ideas. Young children are also quite good at exploring their environment through taste and smell, particularly in relation to their feeding behaviour! The senses of sight, hearing and touch are important for early language development. As the child becomes more proficient the senses of sight and hearing are the two main senses used in literacy and numeracy. If the child shows some difficulties in learning how to read, write or learn numbers, then a 'multi-sensory' approach is often recommended, which means using more than one channel to support learning. This is described in more detail in Chapter 4.

Children make sense of new experiences by relating them to previous learning

The renowned child psychologist, Jean Piaget, developed a theory of children's learning which includes the notions of *assimilation* and *accommodation*. Assimilation is when a child takes in some information from the environment, stores it and uses it as the need arises. Through play the child assimilates or 'gathers in' a great deal of information.

Accommodation is when a 'correction' has to be applied to the original concept or idea as a result of a new experience, and a modification or a change made to a previous view. So children, as they learn new things, build on previous learning experiences. To give an example, if a child wanted a biscuit and the parent had decided to move the place where the biscuits were kept, then the child, not knowing this, would search in the cupboard where, from previous experience, he had learned the biscuits would be. Not finding them, he might give up or, depending on how hungry he was, search other cupboards on the principle that the biscuits would be kept in a similar place. On finding the biscuits he would learn the new location and probably remember it the next time he was wanting a biscuit.

Children who are learning to read are constantly revising their word knowledge. A child who knows the word 'bend' might then apply their learning and be able to recognise 'mend'. A child who knows the word 'cough' might logically pronounce the word 'bough' as 'boff' but would then have to learn that there are a number of ways to pronounce the group of letters 'ough' (i.e. cough, bough, enough, ought).

In learning what numbers are, there is a sequence of prerequisite skills and ideas which need to be in place before the child can do this effectively, e.g. in knowing what 'two' means a child must know it is more than one and less than three and that the word 'two' can be used with any objects where there are two of that object together, i.e. two elephants, two sweets.

In all our learning we build on what we already know. Therefore, in any new learning it is important to gain a knowledge of what the child already knows so that *the next step* can be taught. This raises the importance of the task presented to a child being at the right level. 'If the tasks and activities in which the learner is engaged are not matched to the learner's capabilities, or are not understood by the learner, then learning difficulties are likely to occur' (Ainscow and Tweddle 1988), so it is very important to match the activity to the ability of the child so that a successful learning experience takes place.

Children develop their understanding through talking

If you have ever watched a young child at play you will notice that he or she uses quite a lot of noise and occasionally words alongside their action – it seems to be a natural thing to do. Their play seems first to affect language as children 'commentate' on their actions and then as they grow older language starts to affect play. Much has been written over the years both by philosophers and psychologists about the important relationship between thought and language.

Questions have been asked about how thought affects language and how language guides thoughts and perceptions. It is said, for instance, that the Inuit population have nine different words for 'snow', each of which describes a different sort of snow. Does knowing those words then affect the way they observe and experience snow? If we had the words too, would our perception of snow be enhanced? Both interesting questions. There is undoubtedly a link between understanding language and being able to structure and make sense of our environment and there is evidence that good language structures enable faster and more effective processing of information.

An experiment is described in which young children were presented with a wooden board with holes into which cylinders of different sizes are designed to fit. The experimenters found that children who understood concepts and knew the words for tall/short, fat/thin, wide/narrow were quicker at doing the task than were children who did not seem to understand the words which describe size. The children with an understanding of several size concepts, fat/thin, tall/short, wide/narrow were quicker too than children who understood only big/little as descriptions of size.

These examples demonstrate how language provides a structure for effective thinking. The child who develops language skills without difficulty is likely to go on to learn to read without difficulty and to understand mathematical ideas without difficulty. It is often the children who find it hard to grasp the structure and meaning of language who struggle later with the development of literacy and numeracy skills.

You will note in your work that, for children who do seem to find it harder, a number of them will have been seen by a speech and language therapist at an earlier stage or parents will report that they appeared slow to develop language skills. For some reason, possibly linked to genetic factors, boys are more affected than girls. Many more boys than girls have slow language development in the early years and there are more boys than girls in our schools who require additional support in the area of literacy.

This influence of language on thought processes has considerable implications for your work, as it demonstrates how the need for understanding of basic language skills and concepts have to be in place before the child can learn to read or manipulate numbers. For young children you can check which concepts and ideas they already know and help identify the gaps in their knowledge.

For older children, again you will need to check understanding and not make assumptions that the language concepts necessary for learning a new task are in place.

Children have preferred learning styles and learn at different rates

If you have children of your own, you will be aware that, even for children from similar genetic backgrounds, there are quite marked differences in the ways children develop and learn. Each child has their own personality and predisposition to learning, each their own particular strengths and weaknesses. There is from time to time a debate about the relative influences on our development of 'nature', i.e. what we are born with and 'nurture', i.e. the effects of our families and environment. Most writers accept that it seems to be a combination of both which guides the way we grow, think and learn.

Some of these individual characteristics, especially physical characteristics, appear fixed, e.g. shape of ear, adult shoe size, but some can be influenced by family experience, e.g. a child from a non-nurturing family background may become emotionally disturbed and this will have an effect on how they learn as children who are unsettled in their home lives seem to also find it difficult to 'settle' to learning.

As part of these individual differences, it is recognised that there are different 'learning styles' and by this we mean that there are several channels of communication into a child's mind and we need to determine which one is best for them.

The idea cross references with multi-sensory learning and, in order to identify a child's preferred 'learning style', it is necessary to find out, by observation, trial and error what works best for each child. (See also Chapter 4 for more details on learning styles.)

Children may move across subject boundaries as they learn

Just because literacy is taught in the daily Literacy Hour and numeracy in the daily maths lesson, it does not mean that these skills are not being taught through other subjects or at other times in the child's day. Indeed, you can make links and help children see that, for example, the key words in a history topic are similar to other words used in other lessons, that sentence constructions, layout of work, etc., are common across many subjects. Similarly, ideas of shape, weight, size can be recognised in subjects other than maths and the general skill of classification, useful for all learning, occurs right across the curriculum.

Children learn best when they can make sense of what they do through involvement in planning and reflection

Everyone likes to be involved in planning activities which will affect them. If you were planning an extension to your house you would want to have your views taken into account when the planning was being done because you know what will and what won't work and 'fit' with your style of living. It is the same with learning. Children are much more likely to get the best 'fit' with their learning if you can involve them in planning the work. If they feel they have some control over what they do then they are far more likely to become engaged with the task. Even a simple choice like 'which task shall we do first?' is helpful because the pupil does not feel passive in the process of learning.

This is especially important for pupils experiencing literacy or numeracy difficulties as it is all too easy to 'take a back seat' and let the assistant do it for you. The Literacy Hour, in fact, includes a time for reflection, *the plenary session*, at the end.

The process of reflection on work done, i.e. 'How well did I do it?', 'How might I have done it better?' is also crucial in enabling the pupil to learn. Your role in this is to provide feedback and doing this can be quite a skilled job if the pupil's self-esteem is to be maintained. Children who find literacy and numeracy difficult may be uncertain about their ability to do well, so require plenty of encouragement and reassurance. So it is always important in giving feedback to find something positive to say before asking the child to self-correct their work. If they cannot see what is wrong you will need to point it out using phrases such as 'Jack, you're doing well with this, try putting another 'p' in here, that will make it right'.

Looking at examples of how others have presented work can also be helpful, although it can be de-motivating if the pupil sees work of a standard they think they could never attain!

Children learn through purposeful repetition, practice and reinforcement

If you drive a car, you will recall that there was a time when you could not do it. An intensive period of learning new skills was necessary in order to get to the point where you were ready to drive independently. As you were learning, there was a need for lots of practice, repetition and reinforcement, the 'making stronger' of the correct actions and thinking which combine together to make you into a successful driver. There is also a time element which is significant. If your lessons were six months apart then you would forget a good deal between lessons and would have to start from scratch again. Most learner drivers have lessons at least once a week so that skills can be practised, learned and reinforced. This relates to the way our memories work.

It is acknowledged that there are two types of memory, short-term and long-term, and that, for true learning to take place, information must pass from our short-term memory into our long-term memory and if there is too great a time lapse then this does not happen and learning does not take place.

So it is with the learning of reading, writing, spelling and number skills. Children need to practise these skills often if they are to learn effectively. For children who learn at a slower pace than others this is even more important and much repetition is required for information to 'stick'.

Take the skill of learning to read, which, as we will see later in this book, requires a combination of sub-skills. The majority of children learn to read using a pattern of practice and reinforcement which seems to work. However, there are some children who are subjected to the same 'treatment' who fail to make progress. What is happening? Why don't they learn?

A recent project in Essex called the 'Early Reading Research' project has attempted to change patterns of instruction for children and has shown that certain ways of using repetition, practice and reinforcement can be particularly effective with all children, including children who previously might have had difficulties in learning to read. This particular project has shown that significant improvements in children's reading can be made by using a number of principles which work.

- *Distributed practice* – the researchers found that 'little and often' works much better than longer periods of work at more widely spaced intervals. For children learning to read, short periods of daily practice or even twice daily practice is better than longer periods of work once or twice a week. This is because information in the child's short-term memory is reinforced before it is 'lost' and is therefore more likely to pass into the long-term memory.
- *Interleaved practice* – the researchers also found that learning new words alongside words already learned was more effective than just learning new words alone. This technique seems to help children to remember learned material so the child would, for example, learn 10 words, then another 3, then practice all 13, learn another 3, practice all 16, etc.

Children learn best when there are care, tolerance, security, praise and high expectations associated with clear learning goals

Picture a scene in which a young child is starting to walk. There may be parents or relatives around smiling, clapping, cheering and urging the child on. When the child manages to take the first few hesitant steps, there are celebration and approval and the child gets big smiles from the 'audience'. 'Good boy, now walk to daddy.' If the child were to fall after a step or two, no-one would dream of saying 'No, that's wrong', or 'Get up you lazy boy and do as I say!' So, most adults start off brilliantly as carers and encouragers of children, setting clear expectations of the next step, in this case quite literally! What we need to remember is that children of all ages are learning new skills all the time and they need encouragement at every stage.

Unfortunately, this positive approach seems to fall away for some children as they grow. This sometimes happens as the child becomes more difficult to control or when the adult gets frustrated because the child won't do as he or she is asked. This can happen with learning to read, particularly if the adult working with the child expects too much. It is easy to blame the child sometimes rather than the task or the teacher.

When negative messages are given to a child at an early stage then an unhealthy cycle of 'can't do, won't do' seems to emerge. The child finds it hard to read, the adults give a negative message to the child, the child then thinks negatively of themselves in relation to reading and starts to dislike the experience of reading, viewing themselves as unsuccessful in the task.

The first years at school are important for all children. For those who may be 'at risk' of finding literacy and numeracy difficult, e.g. those who have had some language difficulties at a preschool stage, they are especially important. Particular attention needs to be paid to ensuring that these children do not start to see themselves as failures.

Patience, tolerance and positive regard for children are key qualities of teachers and assistants especially at this important stage of development. (In the previous chapter on 'Giving support' the importance of care, tolerance and praise are discussed in greater detail.) You will need to remember that children constantly need approval and thrive on praise. This can be demonstrated in a number of ways and can be non-verbal, such as a smile, a nod of the head or a pat on the back or it can be verbal, using positive comments about learning behaviour which you observe. Visual feedback is also valuable, particularly for children with poor memories! Tokens of approval such as stars on a chart, 'smiley face' stickers or positive notes home or to the teacher or head teacher can be really effective in motivating the child to learn.

What stops children from learning?

As we have just seen, negative messages to children can hinder their learning by lowering confidence. There are usually several factors which interact to prevent effective learning. These might be:

- negative feedback;
- frequent absence from school;
- limited preschool experience;
- poor language development;
- poor teaching methods;
- expectations too high;
- expectations too low;
- distracting learning environment;
- effect of peer group;
- poor timing of teaching input;
- no recognition of child's preferred learning style.

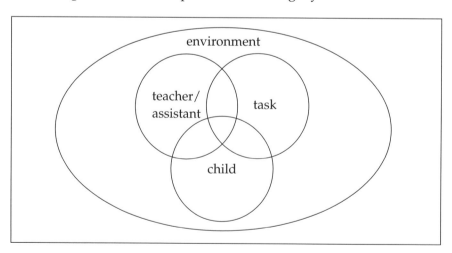

Figure 3.1 Interacting factors in the learning situation

We see then that there are many components to effective learning and interacting factors which need to be considered. Figure 3.1 shows them in diagram form. In more detail the factors are:

- what the child brings – attitude, abilities, prior learning, etc.;
- the nature of the task presented;
- the way the task is taught;
- the learning environment – arrangement of class, peer group, etc.

Imagine that you are given a task to do. The task is to follow a complicated recipe to produce a lemon soufflé within a set time limit. What might stop you from doing this well?

- You haven't got the right ingredients.
- You can't understand the metric weight system.
- You don't like lemons.
- You can't understand some of the instructions (they are translated from a French version).
- Your oven has a fault.
- You don't whip the eggs for long enough.
- The container is too shallow.
- You run out of time.

Let's look at what was stopping you from doing this right and how you might learn to do it better. We need to ask 'What needs to happen for you to do the task successfully?' The answers will vary depending on what prevented you from learning in the first place. Let's assume that you can do this task given the right conditions and support.

Consider the barriers to success and how to remove them:

Barriers to success	Solution
Wrong ingredients	Plan ahead, make sure you have them
Wrong weighings	Ask for a weight conversion table
Don't like lemons	Make a chocolate soufflé
Can't understand instructions	Ask for help
Faulty oven	Arrange to get it fixed
Eggs not whipped enough	Whip eggs for longer
Wrong container	Use a deeper container
Out of time	Learn to work faster or ask for more time

As you will note, the task would have been much easier if some preparations had been made so that the conditions were right for you to be successful. What is also clear in this kind of learning is that a demonstration of how to do this, step by step, would have been particularly helpful.

Consider what would have happened had your soufflé flopped. Most likely you would not view yourself as a successful maker of soufflés and be unwilling to have another go. Your motivation would diminish. If you could have done it but ran out of time you would feel frustrated by the time limit.

Consider too how you would feel if you were making the soufflé in the same room with others who had more success than you. You may feel annoyed or frustrated that others could do this while you could not.

This teaches us that, for learning to be effective: and this applies to all learners:

- Tasks should be demonstrated (have a go yourself!)
- The correct tools for the job need to be prepared.
- Visual prompts can be very useful.
- The preferred learning style should be used.
- Sticking points should be anticipated.
- The rate or pace of learning should be taken into account – allow enough time for success.
- Repetition and practice are needed – work out how much and when.
- Encouragement is essential – we all need it.
- The effects of the environment and peer group need to be considered.

'Show the child how to do it by having a go yourself'

Chapter 4

Supporting children learning to read

The process of learning to read is very complex and we still do not know exactly how every child develops the ability to read despite a vast amount of research. What we do know is that the process follows a developmental pattern and that all children need to develop certain basic skills in order to make progress in any area of learning.

- Focus attention and maintain that focus for several minutes;
- see print adequately;
- sit still for several minutes without being distracted;
- hear, understand and carry out simple verbal instructions;
- remember what is seen or heard for sufficient time to enable the child to respond appropriately;
- want to read and get enjoyment from it.

What do you need to be able to do in order to read?

For many pupils with SEN these pre-requisite behaviours which we so often take for granted may not be well developed for a variety of reasons. If a child cannot sit still, listen, understand what is said and remember for long enough to carry out an instruction, he or she is likely to have severe difficulties in developing basic literacy and numeracy skills. The lack of basic literacy and numeracy skills can then prevent a pupil from being able to access and participate successfully in other areas of the curriculum.

Students understand spoken language, and teachers depend on that. It is from speech that students will come to understand written language as well, provided they have sufficient familiarity with the words and patterns that are to be linked

Marilyn Jager-Adams (1990).

How do reading skills develop?

The development of reading skills is highly dependent on a child developing sufficient language skills.

- They must develop skills in understanding what is said to them and to be able to express their needs, thoughts and ideas in spoken language.
- If children have experience of books and stories are being read to them they begin to develop awareness of books and familiar stories. They begin to understand how books work, e.g. turning pages.
- They begin to recognise and name pictures and show interest in the story, e.g. they can predict what will happen next in a familiar book.
- Children then begin to take notice of print and can begin to recognise their own names or familiar signs in books or shop signs or logos.
- They show interest in active reading and become aware that print goes from left to right, from the top to the bottom of the page. They may begin to recognise some letters by shape and sound.
- Children then begin to read familiar words and to identify initial and final letters in unfamiliar words. They respond to stories they like or dislike.
- Gradually children build up a bank of words they know (often referred to by teachers as sight vocabulary) and can use their knowledge of letter sounds (phonemes) and symbols (graphemes) to begin to attempt unfamiliar words (decoding). They will begin to use the pictures to help them guess unfamiliar words and their knowledge of sentence structure and grammar to modify their guesses.
- As their sight vocabulary increases and they get better at building unfamiliar words through linking the letters (graphemes) to spoken sounds (phonemes) children begin to read more fluently and with expression.
- Later, with more practice and opportunities to read comes fluency and increased accuracy of word recognition and expression through the use of punctuation. As reading becomes more fluent and automatic, understanding (comprehension) of what is read becomes easier.
- Fluent adult readers appear to recognise words effortlessly and to recognise whole words at a glance. Research indicates that 'skilful readers visually process virtually every individual letter of every word as they read whether they are reading single words in isolation or words in connected sentences' (Marilyn Jager-Adams 1990).
- It follows that readers who are unable to recognise individual letters and spelling patterns quickly and without conscious effort are likely to struggle and to not want to read. Often children who find reading difficult, read less and have less practice. Therefore they get further behind their peer group. These are the pupils we often identify as having special educational needs and are likely to be the pupils supported in class by an assistant.
- As an assistant you may be asked to hear children read or share a book with them.

Pupils who find reading difficult to master need more opportunities to practice rather than fewer, but because they find it difficult, they avoid reading rather than want to do it.

Revisiting and re-reading books are very important for practice and are essential elements of the Literacy Hour. Unfortunately they are sometimes viewed by parents as a 'waste of time'!

Re-reading books enables a child to consolidate new skills, practise and learn to recognise new words. It also helps to practise using a variety of cues to decode unfamiliar words, e.g. initial letter sound, cues from the picture plus contextual cues from the sentence structure and meaning of the story. Young children love to re-read familiar stories and it is a most effective way to build confidence as well as practise new skills.

Reading practice and developing reading accuracy

There are two main factors in choosing appropriate books for pupils to read independently.

Firstly, the book must be visually appealing and have the appropriate format. The content must be of interest to the child. Maintaining 'credibility' is very important for older pupils who are struggling with reading. Books need to look like 'real paperbacks' not infant picture books. Some illustrations can put off older children and can lead to pupils rejecting books as 'baby books'. Topics need to be matched to the pupil's age and interests. Boys like to read non-fiction books, often about sport, science, discoveries and cult heroes.

Secondly, books need to be selected at the right level of difficulty to match the child's reading ability.

A good guide is to check that the child can read 80 per cent of the words accurately. If he or she is making more than two errors in every ten words he or she will be reading at frustration level and is likely to either give up or lose confidence. If a child wants to read a particular book that is likely to be above frustration level then 'paired reading' is a good technique. (See below)

How do I know if a book is the right level?

Children need to feel comfortable and not threatened when they are reading. Building confidence by encouragement as well as enjoyment is vital.

- Always look at and discuss the book with the child first.
- Read the title, look at the picture on the cover and discuss what the book is going to be about.
- Flick through the pages glancing at the pictures to get some clues about what happens in the book, unless of course the essence of the book is a surprise ending!

Usually in school, the teacher will select the book to be read. It may have already been read in a Literacy Hour lesson as a whole-class text

What is the best way to hear a child read?

41

or as an assistant you may have to select a book suitable for an individual or group of pupils to read.

Remember that if the children are struggling because it is too difficult, i.e. they are unable to read more than eight out of ten words correctly, you cannot expect them to read independently and a 'paired reading' approach will be necessary.

What is paired reading?

Paired reading is when an adult or another more proficient reader reads aloud at the same time as the child. This method is excellent for parents, grandparents or carers and assistants to encourage reading and is ideal for reading books that are rather too difficult for the child. The child is encouraged to follow the text and to read simultaneously with the skilled reader. In reality, the reader is likely to lag behind fractionally so it is important to adjust the pace so the child can keep up. (You may need to slow down!)

As the child develops confidence he or she is encouraged to indicate, usually by a small gesture, if he or she wants to try reading on their own. The skilled reader then stops reading until signalled to join in again or the child begins to struggle.

This method has been found to be very successful in developing children's reading skills and boosting their confidence. It takes away some of the stress often involved in reading practice where there can be too much emphasis on accuracy.

It also enables pupils with reading difficulties to read books that are of particular interest to them. You can adapt this method to suit the child. You may start reading a sentence and the child finishes the sentence, reading alternate lines or paragraphs. Do whatever works best.

What if the child gets stuck?

When supporting a child reading you often have to look ahead and predict which words are likely to present problems. Usually if a child hesitates it is best just to tell the child any unusual names or irregularly spelt words. If the word is phonically regular (can be sounded out) gently prompt the child to look at the letters and to sound out the (phonemes) letter sounds and to blend them to form the word or syllable. There may be clues in the picture which help the child to recognise the word.

Some children guess wildly and need to be reminded of the context or story to try to make sense of the sentence. Sometimes leaving the problem word and reading to the end of the sentence allows contextual cues to be used to good effect.

What does learning to read involve?

Early on in the development of reading skills children begin to recognise and match written words to names and concepts. For example, many preschool children recognise the familiar signs, e.g. McDonald's Burger Bars, well before they can read anything else.

Some children starting school can recognise their own name before they are able to write it.

The first stages of beginning to read are very visual and involve the recognition of familiar words. In English there are approximately 250 words that make up 75 per cent of all the words we write. These are known as the high frequency words because they are just that – the words we use most frequently.

So when we begin to introduce young children to the words they need to read and write, these are the words we teach them first. We also teach words that are personally important to them, such as their own name, the words 'mum', 'dad', 'home', and names of brothers and sisters and pets, etc. Within the National Literacy Strategy framework there are lists of vocabulary that pupils are expected to be able to read and write. List 1 consists of a list of vocabulary for Reception Year, and Years 1 and 2 and one for Years 4 and 5. Pupils in Year 3 are expected to consolidate the Reception and Years 1 and 2 list before moving on to the Years 4 and 5 vocabulary list (see Appendix B).

Most children will learn to recognise these early words quite easily. The teacher will teach these words a few at a time during shared and guided reading sessions. The children will play games matching the written words to the spoken words, e.g. 'bingo' games. They will practise with short drills where words are written on cards and the pupils have to read the words. The children will use these common words in their own writing with the help of word banks and personal dictionaries.

How do I help pupils develop a sight vocabulary?

While the majority of children soon build up the number of high frequency words they can read and then begin to write, some pupils, particularly those who find reading difficult need more practice before they are able to remember the new words, recognise, and use them.

Flash cards

Flash cards have been used in classrooms for a long time to help children build a sight vocabulary. Target words are written clearly onto a piece of card. The size of the card depends on whether the words are for group or individual use. A picture that begins with that letter stuck on the back of the card will act as a prompt to remind the child of the word. These pictures are particularly effective if they are drawn by the child. Some of the high frequency words such as 'the', 'want', 'have' need to be put into a sentence as a prompt instead of a picture.

Flash cards work well for children who are visual learners but for those who have specific learning difficulties (dyslexia) or other difficulties, a more multi-sensory method of using flash cards can be more effective.

The child is shown the word, says the word, the card is turned over and the child attempts to write it or selects the word from a choice of cards.

A variation on flashcards which is particularly effective and allows individual pupils to work independently on their own word targets, is to use a 'Language Master' recorder. Words are written on cards which have a strip of audio tape along the bottom, so that the pupil (or adult) can record the word. He or she can then see and hear the word simultaneously. To make the activity multi-sensory, the child then turns the card over and writes the word from memory.

Look at word shapes.

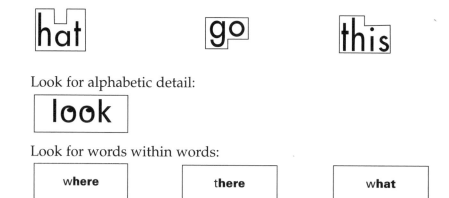

Look for alphabetic detail:

| look |

Look for words within words:

| where | there | what |

To help aid the remembering of the detail of the words, groups of high frequency words can be put together to make simple sentences.

Try to make what can be rather boring learning tasks fun as well as memorable.

Making activities multi-sensory often helps pupils to remember more effectively, and for pupils with dyslexia, multi-sensory approaches are essential.

What are multi-sensory techniques?

These are ways of practising and presenting material so that all the senses are involved. These methods have proved to be very successful with dyslexic children particularly for those with poor memory skills.

Teachers often use multi-sensory approaches when introducing phonics and teaching pupils the links between the grapheme (letter symbol) and the phoneme (sound) it represents. Key Stage 1 teachers in particular will encourage pupils to:

1. *Look* at the shape

2. *Trace* it in the air or sand

3. *Say* the letter sound (phoneme)

4. *Write* the letter.

A multi-sensory approach can be applied to lots of games used in schools to encourage the overlearning of reading and writing words, for instance: bingo games, where pupils have to match given individual words to the words on a card, can be extended by encouraging the pupils to read and then cover the words and then try to write them from memory.

As an assistant working with individual pupils and small groups you will become aware that some children respond better to different games or ways of learning things. Pupils have what is called different learning styles.

How can I recognise the different learning styles of each pupil?

Auditory learners are often quite verbal, they are good at discussions and have a wide range of vocabulary. These pupils tend to work things out or develop ideas by talking about them. Younger children are good at remembering rhymes and songs, they can hear onset and rime and rhythm. They listen attentively and use phonic skills in both reading and writing.

Visual learners often appear well organised and neat in their work. They like to doodle or draw diagrams. They like to get information from pictures and diagrams in books or on computer. They are often quite good at spotting spelling mistakes and proof-reading their writing.

Kinaesthetic learners learn best by doing things. They learn best if they have to do something with the information they have been given, e.g. make a model, or a game, etc. Kinaesthetic learners learn spellings best by writing them.

How can I support pupils to develop phonic skills?

Phonics is a strategy we use to decode the letters in a word. In English we use individual letters and sequences of letters (graphemes) to represent spoken sounds (phonemes) when we write. First, the child has to remember the sound each letter represents (often known as grapheme – phoneme correspondence). Most teachers will target either one or a small group of letter sounds at a time.

The use of short multi-sensory routines can be very helpful for pupils who have difficulty linking and remembering the phoneme associated with each grapheme and vice versa.

These routines can easily be done by making a reading pack of cards consisting of the 26 letters of the alphabet. On the front of each card is a letter, on the reverse is a cue picture, usually of a noun beginning with that word.

Front

Back

The routine:

- Look at the letter.
- Say the letter name.
- Say the letter sound (use picture prompt if needed).
- Say the word (use the picture to prompt if necessary).

This routine can be used for learning digraphs (e.g. sh – ch – th) and trigraphs (e.g. str – scr) in the same way.

Plastic or wooden three-dimensional letters are essential for developing early phonic links with writing and generating words from sounds. The use of an alphabet rainbow is often very helpful for pupils with a poor short-term memory.

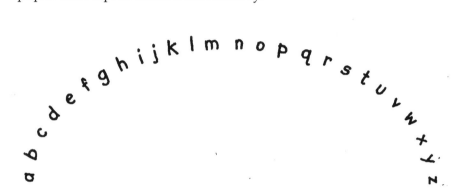

It allows the pupils to see all the letters of the alphabet in sequence easily and enables pupils to match letter sounds to the letters displayed in the rainbow. Plastic or wooden letters can be manipulated to form words. Handling of the three-dimensional shapes helps to reinforce the visual shape of each letter.

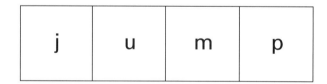

Phoneme frames of three or four boxes on laminated card are excellent for counting phonemes and for sequencing and blending the phonemes in a word:

There are lots of games on the market that are aimed at developing phonic skills. The most effective are those that:

- are easy to play;
- are attractive to look at;
- can be used for a range of activities;
- can be adapted or varied;
- use multi-sensory approaches, e.g. involve looking, reading, saying and doing;
- are fun to play but have clear learning targets.

Existing board games can easily be adapted to support learning targets, e.g. an ordinary snakes and ladders board can be used to help learn new vocabulary or letter sounds by the addition of a set of cards on which are written the letters or words to be learned.

If the child lands on a snake he or she can avoid going down it by picking up and reading the word correctly. This can be adapted to reading or writing a word beginning with the letter shown on the card. If you are playing with the children, they can prevent you from going up the ladders if they pick up a card and answer correctly. Almost any board game can be adapted by attaching different learning activities to the numbers on the dice. For example, if you throw a 1 you must read a word on a card, if you throw a 6 you must spell a word before taking your turn. This can be done with numbers, number bonds, multiplication facts, etc. You will find lots of ideas for phonic activities in the Additional Literacy Support Modules (DfEE 1999a) which can be adapted to match the needs of the pupils you are supporting.

What are phonological skills?

These are a set of aural (listening) skills that children need to develop before they are able to use phonic strategies when reading.

Children usually develop phonological skills in the following order:

- Awareness of whole words as units of sound that have meaning.
- Awareness of rhythm, being able to clap or tap to rhythm.
- Awareness of rhyme – being able to choose a word that rhymes with another.
- Being able to segment spoken words into onset and rime, for example in the word cat – the onset is the /k/ sound the rime is /at/.
- The word boat splits into /b/ as the onset, /oat/ as the rime

  e.g. boat: – b – oat
      dog: – d – og
      chip: – ch – ip.

- Being able to segment words into phonemes:

      cat: – c – a – t
      boat: – b – oa – t
      dog: – d – o – g
      chip: – ch – i – p.

- Being able to generate words that rhyme, e.g. cat – mat – hat – sat.
- Blending phonemes sounds to form words.
- Manipulating the order of phonemes (sounds) to form new words.

Why are phonological skills important in learning to read?

Research on reading now shows that these early skills are essential to the later development of accurate fluent reading. Children who do not develop these skills sufficiently well are likely to have difficulty in learning to read and, later, in developing good fluent writing skills.

What is the difference between phonological skills and phonics?

Phonological skills are a set of skills needed to develop phonic skills. Phonics refers specifically to the linking of letter sounds (phonemes) to letters (graphemes) and how we use this alphabetic coding of sounds in reading and writing.

How can I help to make reading easier?

As an assistant, one of your tasks is likely to be making simple resources and worksheets for individuals or groups of children under the guidance of a teacher.

The following guidelines on design and layout will help to make reading easier.

- Use a simple design and layout.
- Use wide margins and clear spaces between lines and paragraphs.
- Avoid too much writing too close together.
- Use clear fonts, e.g. Sassoon, Plantin, Helvetica, Arial. Avoid Gothic.
- Choose a font size between 12 and 18.
- Avoid the use of upper case letters only. The use of upper and lower case letters helps to make reading easier.
- Avoid overprinting on illustrations.
- Do not use very dark coloured paper, e.g. red, purple, dark blue.
- Pastel coloured paper rather than white helps some pupils.
- When writing worksheets:
  - keep the sentence length short,
  - keep paragraphs short,
  - use bullet points for key facts,
  - avoid using passive mode, e.g. 'put the cake in the oven', *not* 'the cake is put in the oven'.

Chapter 5

Supporting children learning to write

Writing requires the coordination of a large number of senses and movements. For many children the physical act of writing can be difficult for a variety of reasons. Making marks on paper starts off as a rather random activity in very young children with little conscious control or purpose.

By the time most children start school at the age of four they can usually attempt to hold a pencil or crayon and to make marks that begin to show some control and purpose.

- In its earliest stages writing begins to develop from random marks on paper to intentional marks that contain some meaning or children copy the adult behaviour of writing.
- Children then become more aware that writing has meaning and that there is a direct link between speech and writing. Writing is a way of coding speech.
- During these first stages, children may begin to use letter-like shapes and generate writing that looks like words, e.g. short squiggles with spaces in between.
- Children develop an understanding about print and writing, that print goes from left to right, top to bottom down a page.
- Children begin writing with often just one or two key words which then extend to short sentences.
- Then comes the use of punctuation, more complex sentences, wider use of vocabulary.
- Proficient writers are able to write fluently in different styles to match the purpose of their writing. They can spell efficiently, can use punctuation, have a large vocabulary and can communicate well in writing.

How does writing develop?

How can I help a child with poor handwriting?

As an assistant you are likely to be asked to support children who find writing difficult for a variety of different reasons.

During the Literacy Hour the children will be set writing tasks by the teacher during the independent and group work period which usually lasts about 20 minutes. Some children may have weak fine motor control, so that their writing will not be even and fluent. They may have difficulty controlling the direction of the pencil movement and some may have difficulty gripping a pencil or crayon. You can help by encouraging an effective grip using the thumb and forefinger. It is quite acceptable to grip a pencil with the first two fingers on the top. Try to ensure that wherever possible the child grips with the top joint of the thumb and not the base of the thumb.

There are available a number of differently shaped pencils and pens, usually triangular, to prompt a good efficient pencil grip early on. If an older child has developed an unusual grip it is not always possible or advisable to try to change it.

Lines are very helpful because they provide a reference point on which to start. Even as adults we find it quite difficult to write in parallel straight lines on blank paper. Most pads of writing paper contain a guideline sheet at the front. It is even more important for young children to support the development and control of the very fine movements required for writing.

It can be helpful to give a dot as a starting point for a word or letter. The width of guide lines needs to be varied according to the child's own writing and the task to be done.

Often the use of double guide lines helps to promote the difference in height between upper case and lower case letters and lower case letters with and without ascenders. For example:

a b c d e f

Some children may need help with forming individual letters. It is important that in very early writing each child is able to form letters correctly, otherwise the development of joined writing later on becomes a problem. It is particularly important to help children form the following letters correctly:

c o a g d

They all begin with the 'C' shape with the pencil moving from right to left in a curve. If you are using a cursive (joined script) in which a lead in stroke is encouraged, the letter always starts on the line.

- Some children may need to practise forming letters correctly by tracing over examples. As they improve you can gradually fade out the example until each child can start and complete the letter correctly.

- Young children can often improve their motor skills by talking themselves through a sequence of movements. So encourage children to verbalise (quietly) how to form letter shapes.

For the letter a a – 'round up down'.

For the letter m – 'down, back up and over, down back up and over'.
- Small children, just beginning to learn to write, enjoy practising in all sorts of ways by: writing in the air
        in salt or sand
        finger points on a table
        using overwriting felt tip pens
        on whiteboards, chalkboards etc.
- Always try to make the activity multi-sensory by talking through the sequence of movements.
- The letters b and d are often confused. The visual prompt of the word bed can be helpful.
- Encourage the children to close their eyes to form letters and to concentrate on what the movement feels like.
- Dot-to-dot activities, mazes and tracking games are very useful in providing varied opportunities to practise fine motor skills and to develop control and fluency.
- These activities can be varied and made more interesting by using different types of pens, pencils, overwriting felt tip pens ('overwriters', available from most stationers), etc.
- Always be positive but also encourage the children to reflect on what they have done.
- Ask questions such as 'Which is the best letter that you have written?' 'Why is this letter better than that one?' 'How can you improve on this one?' etc., so that the children become aware of, and focus on, the spacing, sizing, shape of letters, words, etc.

How do I help children to improve their writing skills?

For many children, particularly those with specific learning difficulties (dyslexia), there is a gap between their oral language skills and their written language skills. They are not able to express their ideas in writing easily or fluently. You can help in several ways when supporting a group of children engaged in a writing task:

- Some children may just need you to help them spell the occasional words.
- Some may know what they want to write but have only a very limited number of words that they can write independently.
- Provide a bank or list of the most common words that they can refer to. You can always add to the list any specific words that you know the pupils are likely to need for the particular task they have to do.
- Always encourage pupils to try to find the words they need for themselves before you give the word to them.

Some pupils have very little confidence in being able to write anything independently. One effective way to build writing confidence:

- Let the child dictate a sentence to you.
- Write down the sentence on thin card.
- Child reads the sentence aloud.
- Cut up the sentence into words and mix them up.
- Child reconstructs the sentence from the word cards.
- Child selects the words he or she feels confident to write independently and turns these cards over so the writing is hidden.
- Child then writes the sentence.
- Child turns over all the cards and checks.

In this way the amount of copying is reduced to the unfamiliar words and the child builds on his or her own writing vocabulary of the high frequency words.

What is a writing frame?

A writing frame is very helpful in developing writing skills. It is any support that is given to make the writing task easier. Usually a writing frame will help to sequence the content of the writing so that a frame will be a series of headings to help the writer to include all the important elements.

For example, a simple story-writing frame may look like the one shown in Table 5.1.

Table 5.1 A writing frame

Title	What is your story called?
Context	What is it about?
Where	Where does it take place?
Who	Characters
Beginning	Set scene
Middle	What happens?
End	How does the story finish?

How do I help support writing in other areas of the curriculum?

Different subjects of the curriculum have particular writing styles and conventions. One of the more obvious ones is the writing up of science experiments for older pupils. This follows a very clear format with specific headings

Table 5.2 A format for writing up science experiments

TITLE	
Aim	Why did you do the experiment?
Hypothesis	What did you think would happen?
Apparatus used	What equipment did you need?
Method	How did you do the experiment? How did you measure what happened?
Observations	What happened? What did you see?
Results	What results did you get?
Conclusions	Can you explain why you think the results happened?

Support writing with word banks or vocabulary cards containing difficult words, technical words, names of apparatus and chemicals, etc.

The frame shown as Table 5.3, for a formal letter, can be adapted to suit the style of other kinds of letter.

Table 5.3 A frame for writing a formal letter

House number – name of road	
Town	
County	
Post Code	
Date	

Dear Sir or Madam,

I am writing to you because

Do you know that

I would like

I hope that

Yours faithfully,

Do pupils always have to write everything down?

Sometimes children with more severe or complex needs may need to find alternative ways of recording information other than writing. On occasions you may be asked by the teacher to scribe for a child who has difficulty with writing. This is usually done when the thinking is more important than actually producing a piece of writing. Often dyslexic or dyspraxic pupils are limited by their writing skills and cannot demonstrate their real level of ability in a subject by responding in a written form.

A pocket sized tape recorder can be used by pupils to record answers and is often very useful in tests for older pupils. Tape recording is also an excellent medium in which pupils can display their creative writing ability without the restrictions of the writing.

Increasingly, ICT (Information and Communication Technology) is being used in schools for a variety of purposes. Many pupils use computers as a writing resource. There are now lots of software programs that assist with word processing and spelling.

It is important, however, to ensure that students have sufficient keyboard knowledge and speed to use a QWERTY keyboard effectively. Within the next few years the use of the QWERTY keyboard is likely to become less important as voice activated software programs are rapidly improving and becoming much cheaper and easier to use. This software enables the writer to speak directly to the computer, avoiding the necessity of typing. At the present time this software is still being developed to make it easier to use.

When supporting pupils with special needs you constantly have to judge how much to do for the child and how much to encourage them to try for themselves in order to achieve a learning target.

- It is always the class teacher's responsibility to decide what the learning targets are for each child and to plan what the learning outcomes for each lesson will be.
- Always try to plan and discuss with the teacher before the lesson what the content of the lesson will be and what the teacher wants the child or children you are supporting to achieve by the end of the lesson.
- You need to agree with the teacher how you will support the child/children.
- Simply scribing for a child, while he or she dictates, is not always helpful. Scribing may be necessary or desirable in a test situation where the teacher wants to assess how much a child has understood – not how quickly and accurately he or she can write.
- Often pupils are encouraged to use a small, pocket size tape recorder to record what the teacher says instead of trying to take written notes. As an assistant you may be asked to transcribe or write up the notes for a pupil.
- You may need to help a student or group of students by photocopying notes for them.
- Sometimes, particularly in creative writing, pupils will plan their writing on paper and then use a tape recorder.
- If a child's rate of writing is too slow to keep up with the rest of the class you may need to help him or her finish a task before the end of the lesson by scribing for them.
- Always have an agreed system with the class or subject teacher to write on their work to show that you have helped in the writing.
- Homework is often a problem for pupils with special needs. In particular, they may need help to write down clearly the homework to be done in their homework diaries.
- Some students may need photocopied sheets in order to reduce the amount of writing they have to do. For example, in a maths lesson, a photocopied sheet of the sums to be done will avoid the copying of every sum before it can be worked out.
- Comprehension questions can often be transformed into cloze procedures passages, i.e. filling in the missing word in a sentence to reduce the amount of writing needed. For example: *What are the main crops grown in Jamaica?* Can become: *The main crops grown in Jamaica are . . .*

How do I know how much to help a pupil with writing?

Chapter 6

Supporting children learning to spell

Correct spelling is just one element of the writing process, but it is often used as a means of judging the literacy level of individuals.

Spelling, unlike reading, cannot be almost correct. In reading a minor error or substitution has little influence on meaning but spelling is either right or wrong.

In practice it has been found that improving spelling skills is particularly difficult without a great deal of commitment and motivation on the part of the learner. For many children the rewards are not sufficient to motivate them to practise often enough to improve their skills.

What are the best ways of supporting pupils to improve their spelling?

As we have already mentioned there are about 250 words in English that account for about 75 per cent of all the words we write. The National Literacy Teaching framework contains two lists of the words that children need to be able to read out of context and then to learn to spell. (See Appendix B.) Many of these very important words do not follow regular spelling patterns and may need regular practice and reinforcement before children can use them in their writing.

Many pupils, particularly those with specific learning difficulties (dyslexia) have poor short-term memories. They find it difficult to remember what they have seen or heard. Learning spellings can for them be a very boring chore, especially if, despite a lot of practice, they still cannot spell the words. Efforts need to be focused on the most useful and most commonly used words. Any technical words and words related to specific topics can be put onto lists. The number of words to be learned needs to be kept short. It is better to learn one or two words permanently than to attempt too many and not remember any.

A multi-sensory approach, in which all the senses are employed, is always helpful. One of the most effective strategies for learning spellings is the *Look, Read, Cover, Write, Check* procedure. The child:

Looks at the word taking note of all the letters;
Reads the word aloud;
Covers up the word;
Writes the word from memory;
Checks to see if the attempt is correctly spelt;
If it's wrong – tries again!

In order to ensure that the words are remembered permanently, they need to be practised several times a day if possible, until the child is able to use them spontaneously in his or her writing. Unfortunately, spelling a word correctly in the weekly spelling test is not a good indicator of permanent learning!

Simultaneous Oral Spelling (SOS) is another method that can be added to the *Look, Read, Cover, Write, Check* procedure so that it becomes:

Look at the word;
Read the word aloud;
Spell the letter names aloud;
Cover the word;
Write the word at the same time as spelling out the letter names;
Check.

Neurolinguistic Programming

A process known as *Neurolinguistic Programming* has been found to be an effective strategy for older pupils. This strategy is a mainly visual approach to spelling which focuses on the fact that good spellers use the upper left visual quadrant to fix their eyes to both file and recall words. A recent research report by the Helen Arkell Dyslexia Centre (DfEE 1999a) indicates that this method is probably the most effective strategy. They found that if children were encouraged to close their eyes and to move the eyes upwards and to the left they had more success at visualising the word.

A Neurolinguistic spelling routine would be:

- Write the word on a piece of paper or card.
- Close your eyes and think of something that makes you feel successful or good.
- Open your eyes and look at the spelling.
- Move the word on the card upwards and to your left.
- Remove the card but try to keep on 'seeing' the word.
- Look at the word again with the card in the upper left hand position.
- Remove the card and write down the letters of the word you are 'seeing' when you look up and to the left.
- Look at the word you have written. Try to decide if your version is correct.
- Check the word.

- If it is not correct, repeat the process.
- It has been found to be helpful to pupils if the teacher writes the target words to be learned on the top left hand corner of the blackboard.

The use of a Language Master recorder (Drake Educational) is an ideal way to promote the multi-sensory overlearning of spellings. The word is written onto a card which has a strip of audio tape along the bottom. The card is placed in the Language Master and the child can record the word onto the tape. The child can then develop the multi-sensory sequence into:

Look
Read
Hear
Spell out (orally)
Cover
Write
Check

The use of a Language Master is highly motivating even for older pupils who will work independently on practising their spellings for short periods.

Mnemonics

Mnemonics can be used very effectively for words that prove to be very difficult for a child to remember. There are some well known mnemonics for some words that are difficult to remember. For example: *because*

Big Elephants Can't Always Use Small Exits

Big Elephants Can't Always Use Small Exits

Mnemonics tend to work best when the child has developed their own personal mnemonic, if they are funny and are easy to visualise. Always encourage the children to draw a picture to illustrate the mnemonic.

Syllables

Some words are difficult to spell because the pronunciation does not match the spelling, for example: *was, Wednesday, people*.

We can help remember these words by emphasising the way a word is spelt.

For example: We say *woz* but we write *w-a-s*

We say *Wensday* but we write it *Wed-nes-day*

We say *peeple* but we write it *pe-o-ple*

Breaking words into syllables helps focus on the spelling pattern.

You can make up simple card games to reinforce the concept of syllables by cutting up words into syllables and then collecting the syllables to make words.

Looking for words within words can also help children pay attention to the way the word is spelt.

For example: *together – to-get-her*

Saturday – Sat-ur-day

carpet   – car-pet

How can I support older pupils to improve their spellings?

- Scanning text
  Scanning activities help pupils focus their attention on the visual pattern of spellings. Word searches are very popular with most children, either on a computer or paper.
  Children are fascinated by the way the word they are searching for almost 'jumps out' of the page.
- Remind the children to look carefully at the word and to try to visualise it in their minds before they start to search.
- Scanning through books or magazines for a word or spelling pattern and then highlighting the words with a pen is a good activity to promote attention to the spelling patterns within a word. It also helps to develop scanning skills needed for proof-reading and when searching for information in a text.
  For older pupils, scanning texts for spelling patterns is a useful activity to illustrate the variety of spelling patterns that are used to represent the same sound. For example:
  /*a*/eight, ate, wait, delay
  /*e*/meet, meat, receipt
  /*i*/fight, bite, apply, pie

- Scanning texts can also lead older pupils to becoming aware of which spelling patterns are used most commonly to represent a sound. For example,
  ai is more common than *ay*
  ea is more common than *ee*
  ow (as in own) is more common than *oa* (as in boat)

What can I do to help pupils with spelling words they cannot learn or remember

- *Proof-reading:* going back and checking your work for errors is an essential element of any written task. Many pupils who are poor spellers find this quite daunting and will often miss out the proof-reading stage. They may even expect you to do it for them! You can help by providing vocabulary lists of the technical or subject specific vocabulary that they may need. Encourage them to highlight words that 'look wrong' to them even if they cannot correct the words.
- There are aids to spelling such as hand-held spellcheckers and using a spellchecker on a word processor or computer. Unfortunately, spellcheckers will not always recognise a pupil's attempts at spelling a word. Spellcheckers work best with students who can produce spellings quite close to the correct version. Some students whose spelling is very weak will not find them helpful at all.
- Encourage pupils to write a first draft without too much attention to spelling so that the flow of ideas is not interrupted.
- Advise pupils to spell phonetically in tests and exams – (how the word sounds). In this way the reader is more likely to understand a word that is not correctly spelt.
- Remember that even in public examinations such as GCSE and 'A Levels', spelling is not marked in all subjects. Where marks are awarded for spelling, punctuation and grammar the percentage is very small and students should be encouraged to counteract any marks lost for poor spelling by focusing on gaining extra marks for the content of their answers.

Are dictionaries helpful to poor spellers?

Anyone who is a poor speller and has tried to use a dictionary to help will know its limitations. You need to be able to spell a word accurately in order to look it up in a conventional alphabetic dictionary.

Pupils can be helped to find their way around a dictionary by learning to divide the dictionary into quarters.

A B C D E F G H I J K L M N O P Q R S T U V W X Y Z

Pupils should be encouraged to focus on the initial letter of the word and its position in the alphabet.

- Opening the dictionary at the middle will find M.
- The middle of the front half of the dictionary will find words beginning with F.
- The middle of the final half of the dictionary will find words beginning with S. Thus you can help pupils avoid scanning through a large number of pages to find a word that begins with a letter towards the end of the alphabet. This cuts down the amount of search time.
- There are on the market a number of 'spelling dictionaries' which some students find helpful and there is a more specialised dictionary which is aurally coded so that the words are organised according to how they sound and not how they are spelt. In this dictionary you can look up the word *rhinoceros* assuming it to begins with '*ri*' or *physician* as if it begins '*fis*' and find it. Many students and adults have found this dictionary, known as the ACE (Aurally Coded English) Spelling Dictionary (Moseley and Nichol 1986), helpful at school and work.

What can I do to help pupils who cannot use a dictionary?

Some of the pupils you will be supporting will not be able to use a commercially published dictionary because their ability to scan through lists of words is weak and they may not even recognise the word they are looking for. You can help these pupils in a number of ways:

- Word cards with a picture prompt to help recognition of the word. Sets of word cards linked to particular topics or activities can be very useful if kept in plastic wallets or containers.
- Personal dictionaries are helpful for many children with reading and writing difficulties. A personal dictionary can be made from a notebook in which an alphabetic index has been cut down the right hand side. Key vocabulary can be written in the book and then words added as the child needs them. It is often helpful to group words together by topic so that number words are on one page or months of the year are together, etc.

Computers can help in a number of different ways.

Can computers help poor spellers?

- Word processing software will contain a spellcheck facility, but some programs will not recognise the incorrect words and may suggest alternatives bearing no relationship to the word attempted. Some programs will underline spelling mistakes as the text is typed. This can be distracting for pupils. If this is the case it may be better to turn off the spellchecker and then to spellcheck the work at the end.

- There are lots of educational programs that are designed to help pupils with spelling. The best are those that have different levels of difficulty and allow personal word lists to be added.
- Computer spelling programs provide an excellent multi-sensory way to encourage pupils to overlearn by frequent practice the high frequency vocabulary and other irregular words.
- In recent years voice-activated software is being used increasingly in schools. It is becoming more 'user friendly' but still requires the user to read a large number of quite complex sentences. Some pupils may struggle to read and articulate these. Nevertheless, it seems that this type of software, linked to a word processing program, is likely to make the need for accurate spelling and typing less vital for both pupils and teachers in the future!

© Martin Rowson '99

Chapter 7

Giving support in the Literacy Hour

The National Literacy Strategy framework for teaching introduced in 1998 sets out the teaching objectives for all children from Reception to Year 6 to enable pupils to become literate.

The term literacy includes the skills of reading and writing as well as speaking and listening to enable pupils to understand and use oral and written language.

What is literacy?

By the end of the Reception year most children should have a good understanding of the concepts of print and be able to speak clearly, retell stories and have started to develop the early skills of reading and writing. The full details of these Early Learning Goals are given in Appendix C.

What should literate pupils be able to do?

According to the National Literacy Strategy framework (DfEE 1998a), literate pupils should:

- Read and write with confidence, fluency and understanding.
- Be able to use a full range of reading cues (phonic, graphic, syntactic, contextual) to monitor their reading and correct their own mistakes.
- Understand the sound and spelling system and use this to read and spell accurately.
- Have fluent and legible handwriting.
- Have an interest in words and their meanings.
- Understand and be able to write in a range of genres in fiction and poetry.
- Understand, use and be able to write a range of non-fiction texts.
- Plan, draft, revise and edit their own writing.
- Have a suitable technical vocabulary through which to understand and discuss their reading and writing.

- Be interested in books and read with enjoyment.
- Through reading and writing develop their powers of imagination, inventiveness and critical awareness.

Will all pupils be able to achieve the National Literacy Strategy objectives?

This list is quite a tall order for the average adult but many 11 year old pupils will find it very difficult to successfully master all the requirements set out in the National Literacy Strategy. Many pupils will require encouragement and support from both school and home to reach just some of the literacy objectives.

Children who find learning difficult will require support and help to establish and develop some essential skills that are prerequisite to learning such as being able to sit still and listen to instructions, and to remember instructions for sufficiently long to be able to carry them out.

For some pupils the teaching objectives in the framework may be too difficult and they may need to work on targets set for younger children. Some children will need extra teaching and support in order to master some of the objectives which they find particularly difficult.

What is a Literacy Hour?

The Literacy Hour aims to provide a daily period of literacy teaching for all pupils. The National Literacy Strategy framework specifies what should be taught. The Literacy Hour specifies how the teaching is delivered. Teachers are expected to use a wide range of teaching strategies and styles within the Literacy Hour to ensure that pupils remain motivated and interested throughout. The diagram (Figure 7.1), shows the prescribed structure for the hour.

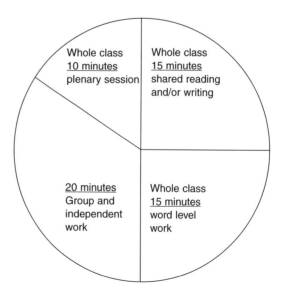

Figure 7.1 The structure of the Literacy Hour

The Literacy Hour is made up of several activities

1. *Approximately 15 minutes* of whole-class teaching from a shared text. For pupils at Key Stage 1 this is usually a 'big book' which the teacher reads with the class, focusing on comprehension: word building, modelling the use of different cues to identify unfamiliar words and to check for meaning. These sessions are known as shared reading sessions and enable the teacher to help pupils in the reading of texts that may be at a level above their normal level of independent reading.

   For pupils at Key Stage 2 the shared reading session may be used by the teacher to extend the reading skills of pupils. The session may be used for whole-class shared writing in which the teacher uses texts to provide models and ideas for writing. In working with the class, the teacher may model how to compose text, and demonstrate how to plan, sequence and compose written text. Shared writing can also be used to teach spelling and grammar.

2. *Approximately 15 minutes whole-class word level work.*
   Word level work refers to some of the subskills that need to be mastered in order for reading and writing skills to progress. Phonics and spelling are emphasised. Word recognition of common words and new vocabulary is also taught in these sessions.

   At Key Stage 2 the emphasis shifts from phonic skills to spelling rules, grammar and punctuation.

3. *Approximately 20 minutes of guided group or independent work.*
   This session provides an opportunity for the teacher to work with a smaller group of children for a period of guided reading or writing while the rest of the class works independently either individually, in pairs or groups.

4. *The final 10 minutes of the Literacy Hour is a whole-class plenary session.*
   The teacher can re-emphasise the main teaching points of the lesson and can assess the progress of the pupils during the lesson. It also allows the pupils to discuss, reflect on and revise new skills or information that they have been using during the lesson.

   Often the texts used during the Literacy Hour are from other areas of the curriculum, e.g. science, history or geography but the emphasis throughout the hour is on the explicit teaching of reading and writing.

   Most pupils will also need additional time during the week to practise reading and independent reading skills. Older pupils will also need additional time for extended writing activities.

What is the Additional Literacy Support Programme?

The Additional Literacy Support (ALS) Programme has been designed to help those pupils in Years 3 and 4 who have begun to fall behind in literacy but are not already receiving extra support. The 24 week programme has been designed to be delivered by classroom assistants and teachers working together in partnership. It is a programme of targets, activities and resources that will help the pupils consolidate many of the Key Stage 1 targets. It consists of four, eight-week modules; each module covers:

- Phonics that have not been mastered at Key Stage 1.
- Reading – both guided and supported to help the pupils become fluent and accurate in their reading.
- Writing – shared and supported, in which pupils use word and sentence level skills in their writing.

Every pupil will cover three modules in the 24 week period. Each week the programme will consist of three 20 minute group work sessions taken by the classroom assistant and one 20 minutes session delivered by the class teacher.

What does it mean for children who struggle?

The Literacy Hour is designed to provide clear guidelines on the time and class management for teachers but there will be a number of pupils in every class who will need additional support and differentiated tasks and teaching during the Literacy Hour. It is acknowledged that a significant number of pupils will need additional teaching to consolidate the word level targets. In particular, the phonics targets have been identified as an area of difficulty for many pupils. Funding has been made available to schools for pupils attaining level 2C in writing in the Key Stage 1 SATS.

How will children with special educational needs cope in the Literacy Hour?

For many Key Stage 1 pupils with Special Educational Needs the structure of the Literacy hour is likely to prove very demanding. The need for pupils in the early years to sit and listen to the teacher for up to 30 minutes can prove to be a problem. Some pupils with severe difficulties may find it impossible to participate in a whole-class session for more than a few minutes. Some pupils may only be able to participate for a few minutes with support from an assistant. The aim should always be for the pupil to gradually extend his or her participation in the whole-class session.

Some pupils may need to be working towards the mastery of literacy objectives that are set for younger children. *For example,* pupils in Years 4 or 5 may still need to revise and consolidate some of the word level targets, in particular the phonic targets, set for Year 2. Some pupils in Years 4 or 5 may not have fully mastered the reading and spelling of all the high frequency words in List I of the National Literacy Framework. Pupils in Year R or Year 1 may not be ready to recognise rhyme and may need to develop recognition of rhythm first.

As an assistant in a school, you may be part of a large learning support team consisting of several teachers and assistants led by the Special Needs Coordinator (SENCO), or in a small school you may be the only support assistant working with the SENCO and class teacher.

Learning support in its widest sense is provided by all teachers to all pupils. All class teachers have responsibility for planning the learning programmes and monitoring the progress of all pupils in their class.

What is my role in the Literacy Hour?

How can I support appropriate behaviour in the Literacy Hour?

Some children will find it difficult to concentrate or to behave appropriately for prolonged periods during the whole-class session. You can help them to extend their concentration and to refocus their attention if it wanders in different ways, such as:

- A quiet verbal prompt, e.g. 'Look at the book'.
- A gesture, e.g. pointing to the relevant line on the page.
- Being able to make eye contact with pupils is often very important so that you can send non-verbal messages by facial expressions to prompt them back to what they should be doing.
- At the end of each session always praise the efforts of the children for concentrating and behaving appropriately even if they were not completely successful.
- Class teachers will often have a reward system, of stickers or points etc., to encourage positive behaviour. Be sure to find out how the system works so that you can also use it.

Shared reading takes place during Literacy Hour when the class teacher shares the reading of a book or text, usually a big book, with the whole class. The aim of shared reading is for the teacher to choose a book that is above the independent reading level of most of the class in order to demonstrate to the class different early reading skills, for example:

What is shared reading?

- Reading from left to right across the page.
- Teaching and practising phonic word recognition skills in context.
- Identifying sentence structure and the use of punctuation.
- Demonstrating other reading strategies such as:
  - use of context
  - self checking for meaning

Shared reading usually takes place during the first 15 minutes of the Literacy Hour. As an assistant you may be asked to lead a shared reading session with an individual pupil or small group of pupils who find reading difficult. If possible, try to observe a number of different teachers taking a shared reading session so that you can observe the range of styles and emphases that different teachers use in these sessions.

If you are unsure about what you have to do, always ask!

What is guided reading?

Guided reading usually takes place in small ability groups (usually about six pupils) within the third part of the Literacy Hour lasting for about ten minutes. In this session the pupils read individual books often from a graded reading scheme. The teacher will match the set of books chosen with the reading abilities of the group, usually with some degree of challenge so that they can be read independently with support from an adult.

The aims of the session are to support the children in using a range of reading strategies including:

- the use of phonic skills;
- using picture cues;
- checking that what they read makes sense using grammar and context to help identify words accurately;
- correcting their own errors.

As an assistant, check with the teacher which strategies or teaching points he or she wishes you to focus on. The guided reading session enables pupils to apply what they have been taught in the shared whole-class session together with skills such as phonics, which they have practised in the independent group work or in a supported reading session.

It is quite usual for an assistant to be asked to take a guided reading session with a small group of pupils either as part of a Literacy Hour or as an extra reading session for pupils who may need additional practice to help improve their reading skills.

What is independent reading?

Independent reading is the third type of reading session that takes place in the Literacy Hour. As the title suggests, individual pupils have the opportunity to read independently either silently or aloud during the third part of the Literacy Hour or at other times during the day. Many schools timetable specific times of the day for whole classes, even the whole school, to devote time to independent reading. During these sessions fluent readers may read a book of their own choice or one suggested by the teacher. Early readers or those pupils with special educational needs are likely to be reading a book from a graded reading scheme or to be re-reading a book already read in a previous guided or shared reading session. As an assistant you may be asked to support pupils who find it difficult to read independently so that this session will be a guided reading session for them.

Often as an assistant you will be asked to support an individual group of children during the independent or group work session. You need to be clear what the task is and what outcomes the teacher wants from the session. You may need to:

- remind pupils about the main features and examples from the shared text;
- repeat the teacher's instructions;
- ask the children to tell you what they have to do;
- prompt them to think how they are going to do it and what apparatus, books, equipment, etc. they need to help them do the task;
- remind the children of the purpose of the task and the end product.

Key things to remember when supporting writing are:

- To support and scaffold the activity – not to do it for the child. Avoid just writing for the child
- Use questions to guide the child to the next stage of the task with questions like:
  – What have you got to do first?
  – What will you need to help you . . . ?
  – Are there any words you will need that you cannot spell?
  – Where did it happen?
  – What happened next?
  – Who did that? etc.
- Try to avoid telling a child what to write.

Multi-sensory and scaffolding techniques, as described in Chapters 4, 5 and 6, can be used to ensure that all pupils whatever their learning style can benefit.

How do I support writing in the Literacy Hour?

During the plenary session of a Literacy Hour the class teacher will revisit and re-emphasise the main objectives of the lesson.

- You can support pupils by encouraging them to respond to the teacher's questions.
- Prepare with your group before the plenary by reminding them of what they have done and what they have learnt during the lesson.
- Help the children to write or draw prompt cards with key words or facts written on them.
- For children with language or communication difficulties translate their signing or use of symbols for the rest of the class.
- Always reinforce and repeat the teacher's praise and comments to a group or individual.
- Tell the teacher and the class of any individual achievements or successes in the group you have been supporting.

How can I give support in the plenary session?

Chapter 8

Supporting children's numeracy skills

What is numeracy?

The dictionary definition of numeracy is 'the ability to use numbers especially arithmetical operation' (*Collins English Dictionary* 1991).

The National Numeracy Strategy (1999b) states that: 'Numeracy is a proficiency which involves confidence and competence with numbers and measures'. The Numeracy Strategy lists the skills that a numerate pupil should possess:

- have a sense of the size of a number and where it fits into the number system;
- know by heart, number facts such as number bonds, multiplication tables, doubles and halves;
- use what they know by heart to figure out answers mentally;
- calculate accurately and efficiently, both mentally and with pencil and paper, drawing on a range of calculation strategies;
- recognise when it is appropriate to use a calculator, and be able to do so effectively;
- make sense of number problems, including non-routine problems, and recognise the operations needed to solve them;
- explain their methods and reasoning using correct mathematical terms;
- judge whether their answers are reasonable and have strategies for checking them where necessary;
- suggest suitable units for measuring and make sensible estimates of measurements;
- explain and make predictions from the numbers in graphs, diagrams, charts and tables.

Most adults would find this list quite a tall order but these skills are expected of our 11 year old pupils. Obviously, many of the pupils you are supporting will not achieve all of these skills by the age of 11 and a few may only begin to achieve some of the skills of numeracy.

The development of the concept of number goes through a number of developmental stages which are dependent on several factors such as:

- being able to see and hear sufficiently well;
- having sufficient short-term memory to remember what is seen and heard;
- having opportunities to experience concrete activities with number;
- having sufficient language skills to develop a range of mathematical vocabulary and to understand the underlying concepts of mathematical activities;
- being able to understand mathematical concepts and to apply them to a wide range of situations and problems.

Language is essential to the development of numeracy and mathematical skills and underpins our understanding of new concepts. Learning in maths involves the acquisition and understanding of mathematical language. In the early stages of mathematical development, children have to learn the concepts of number, the classification and ordering of objects, pattern recognition, quantity, size, etc., and the language that describes these concepts.

There are lots of everyday words that when used in a maths context have a very different meaning – which can be very confusing!

e.g.
cycle	prime
even	product
factor	relationship
foot	root
mass	score
mean	share
odd	take away
order	table
place	times

So you may need to help children translate mathematical vocabulary appropriately and to help them to understand the new meaning of a word within the context of a maths lesson.

Mathematical language can be very precise or very variable. The sum 6 + 2 = 8 can be expressed in lots of different ways:

6 add 2 is 8
6 add 2 equals 8
6 and 2 equals 8
2 and 6 is 8
2 added to 6 gives 8
6 plus 2 equals 8
The total of 2 and 6 equals 8

The sum 8 − 2 = 6 could be expressed as:

8 take away 2 equals 6
8 minus 2 is 6

What are the factors that can affect the ability of pupils to learn maths?

Subtract 2 from 8 equals 6
8 subtract 2 equals 6
6 is 8 minus 2
6 is 2 less than 8
If you take 6 from 8, 2 is left
The difference between 8 and 6 is 2
2 less than 8 is 6

- It is important that children are exposed to the variety of language in maths and to the different meanings in a variety of different ways.

PARTITION	TESSELATE
VERTEX	CUBOID
INTEGER	TALLY

- Most children begin to understand about number and counting by experiencing number in concrete practical ways, by counting, grouping, ordering real objects.
- Children need to manipulate numbers in flexible ways, for example:
  (a) to be able to count forwards or backwards;
  (b) to recognise clusters of objects without ordering the objects.

Lack of this flexibility can lead to a delay in acquiring complete understanding and consistent use of number by children (Sharma 1990). The variety of vocabulary used in maths is very wide. As adults we are inclined to use words like 'add', 'plus' 'and' interchangeably because we know that in maths they all mean the same thing but for children it can be very confusing. Figure 8.1 shows the range of alternative vocabulary linked to the four operations.

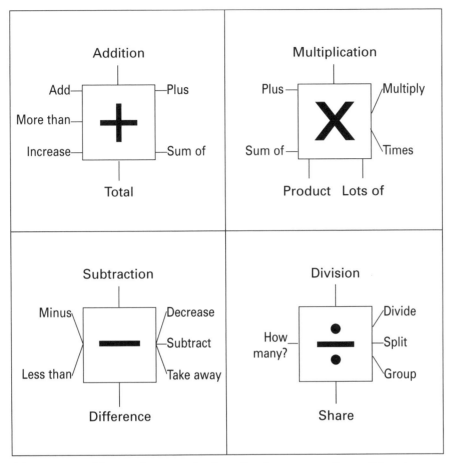

Figure 8.1 Alternative vocabulary for four operations (Henderson 1989)

When you are supporting pupils in a maths lesson, they may need help, not just in reading the problem but in interpreting the vocabulary in the problem in order to decide which of the four operations (add, subtract, multiply, divide) they have to do. Dyslexic pupils will not only have difficulty reading the questions but may also be confused by the vocabulary. The diagram in Figure 8.1 will help by acting as a reminder.

- The language of mathematical questions often poses problems for older pupils with dyslexia if the question is not direct and obvious and is embedded in the text.

  For example:
  (a) How much older is John than Philip? Philip is 17 years old and John is 19 years old.
  (b) In England we can learn to drive at 17 years old. How many years will it be before Sam, who is 9 years old, can learn to drive?

You can help pupils by simplifying questions, translating some of the terms used or rephrasing the questions so that the child can understand which of the four mathematical operations is required.

How do children develop number concepts?

Much of our understanding of the development of number in children is based on the work of Piaget from the 1950s. Sharma (1990) describes four stages in the development of number concepts based on the Piagetian stages of number conservation.

Stage 1

Can recognise groups of one, two or three objects without counting.

Can distinguish between large and small collections of objects and is developing the concepts of *larger* and *smaller*.

Can distinguish between *larger* and *smaller* collections of any size if they are lined up to show one to one correspondence.

Stage 2

Can begin to count objects correctly. At this stage the child does not connect the final number in the counting sequence as representing the total size of the collection for numbers greater than five.

Stage 3

Can count to determine the size of a collection but does not recognise, for example, that eight is more than seven. At this stage the child begins to recognise the number of objects in a small group (up to four) without counting.

Can understand that by counting one can name the number of objects in a collection.

Stage 4

Can recognise the larger set of objects for numbers up to ten. They have a consistent ability to count accurately.

How can I help children learning to count?

As we have already suggested, developing counting skills successfully needs lots of practice with real objects. Usually small objects such as cubes, beads, counters, plastic animals, cars, etc. are used in school. Learning to count is not just the meaningless repetition of a sequence of words.

- Children have to learn that each number word has an explicit consistent meaning – that the word two has the same meaning whether it refers to two cats, two biscuits, two pencils, two cars, two books, two legs etc.
- Children need opportunities to sort varieties of objects into small number sets. This can be done into boxes, trays, hoops, etc. using a variety of everyday objects or commercially produced 'mathematical resources'.
- From about the age of two to three children will hear and imitate counting sequences in rhymes and songs.
  Children may need help to separate the sounds into individual words, each with a unique meaning and a fixed order.
- Finger games and rhymes such as '1, 2, 3, 4, 5, once I caught a fish alive', 'Five currant buns in a baker's shop', etc. encourage counting. There are lots of counting rhymes and songs but actions using fingers, pointing to a number line or cards will help separate the words in the sequence to become meaningful.
  So when singing songs or rhymes always try to include a concrete action such as holding up number cards, the correct number of fingers or use props or pictures to make the links between the number word and meaningful objects or number symbols.
- Children need to be able to count backwards and to count on from a given number.
- The use of concrete apparatus such as number lines and number squares are invaluable in helping to remember the sequence of the numbers.

We know that there are certain skills and behaviour that are essential to ensure that pupils are able to learn, e.g. being able to sit still, listen, focus their attention, etc. In mathematics there are certain skills that are essential to enable effective learning to to take place.

Sharma (1981) believes that children may have learning difficulties in mathematics if they have not developed a range of skills which are needed to support maths learning. These so called prerequisite skills include:

- *Classification of objects*
  – being able to group objects or information according to a specific feature or attribute.
- *Matching and one-to-one correspondence*
  – the beginning of counting and numeracy;
  – being able to match one set to another set.
- *Ordering and sequencing*
  – being able to arrange objects by comparing and relating them to a given attribute, for example, sorting a set of shapes into order of height or size.
  – being able to follow a set of instructions in order.

What skills do children need to support the development of numeracy skills?

75

- *Spatial organisation*
  - to be aware of spatial relationships, e.g. to recognise the difference between 23 and $^2/_3$.
- *Visualisation*
  - to be able to hold and manipulate numbers in your head, e.g. mental maths calculations.
- *Pattern recognition*
  - children need to be able to see patterns in mathematical information.
- *Estimation*
  - the ability to predict the outcome of an activity;
  - to be able to estimate the answer to a sum or problem.
- *Deductive thinking* is the ability to recognise the connection between examples and a rule or formula in order to solve a problem.
- *Inductive thinking* is the ability to take several examples and arrive at a general principle.

Children have different individual learning styles in maths as well as literacy. The learning style will affect how a child makes sense of mathematical information and which strategies he or she can use effectively. Sharma refers to *quantitative* and *qualitative* learners but Chinn and Ashcroft (1998) call then *'inch worms and grasshoppers'*. The quantitative learners are the 'inch worms' who prefer a step-by-step procedural approach to maths. They may be able to follow the procedure and get sums right but do not always understand the maths concept. Qualitative learners or 'grasshoppers' are better at seeing patterns and relationships but they are not so good at following procedures accurately. They often understand the concept but tend to miss out the detail. They can often estimate well but get calculations wrong because of seemingly careless errors.

With whole class teaching the teacher needs to be aware of the needs of the different learning styles of the pupils by giving lots of examples, looking for and generating the rule or principle and then practising more examples.

How do I know how best to help a child?

- As an assistant you need to be aware of the different learning styles children may have. The 'inch worms' or quantitative learners may be able to get the sums correct but may not always understand what they are doing or be able to apply a rule in 'real life' situations. They may need help to recognise what type of operation they have to do to solve a problem, e.g. 'Susan is 17 and John is 4 years younger than Susan. How old is John?' This is a subtraction problem, i.e. $17 - 4 = 13$.
  Qualitative learners or 'grasshoppers' may often appear careless, e.g. missing out a decimal point, forgetting to include a digit in the calculation. They will need encouragement to set out sums accurately and to check their answers carefully.
- Some children may need help to read written maths problems

because their reading skills are weak. Other children who can read the problems may need help in interpreting the problem into mathematical calculations and in deciding which mathematical operations are needed to solve the problem.

- Ask questions that guide the child to think and make estimations about the answer they would expect. Help them to decide whether to add or subtract; multiply or divide.

As we discussed earlier, some children may need help linking specific vocabulary such as *total*, *product*, *difference* and which operations they refer to (see page 73). A chart on the wall or stuck in a maths exercise book will help a child learn mathematical vocabulary.

- Children may have a particular difficulty with writing and fine motor skills. They cannot write numbers easily or have difficulty writing sums with the figures in line with each other.
  The use of squared paper or exercise books can be very helpful particularly for dyspraxic pupils but the squares must not be too large or too small.
- For students with more severe fine motor skill difficulties or severe visual memory difficulties it may be more appropriate to provide a pre-printed worksheet which avoids the problem of copying and setting out sums accurately. As an assistant you may be asked to prepare or photocopy worksheets in advance of the lesson.
- Care needs to be taken in prepared work sheets to allow sufficient space in which to write the answer bearing in mind any writing difficulties. Worksheets also need to provide sufficient space for

'You asked me to take one away!'

informal jottings that may be needed to work out the answer. The same guidelines apply to preparing maths worksheets as to English worksheets in order to make them easier to read (See Chapter 4).

- Pupils who find learning difficult may need to practise counting and ordering numbers using practical apparatus such as counters, cubes and other small apparatus. They may also need to have access to number lines or a number square because they cannot easily hold numbers in their heads.
- Personal number lines can be folded and stuck in the back or front of an exercise book so that a pupil can use them whenever he or she needs to.

In the same way a number square or multiplication square can be stuck into the back or front of an exercise book so that it can be unfolded and used even when the pupil is writing in the book.

For right handed pupils it is better to stick number lines or squares inside the front cover and for left handed students inside the back cover so the writing arm does not cover the number square or line.

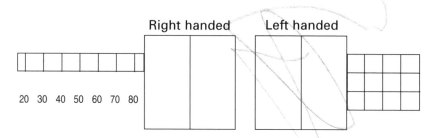

Figure 8.2 Number squares

Children who have difficulty with spatial organisation and orientation are not always aware that it is not only important to recognise and use the correct numbers but the relative position of numbers is also important. In particular, the concept of place value is dependent on the order in which numbers are written. The child needs to understand that:

- 3108 is quite different in value to 1038;
- 0s are important and need to be written in the correct place;
- 23 is not the same as 2/3, and 34 is not the same as 3/4.

You may need to point out to a child and let the child practise noticing the differences and being able to write correctly some of the conventions of mathematical notation.

Partitioning or place value cards are very useful to practise partitioning (dividing a number into its constituent values), e.g. 368 is 3 hundreds 6 tens 8 units.

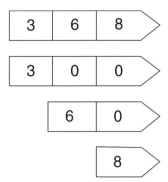

Figure 8.3 Place value cards

- To enable children to visualise and to recognise patterns in numbers, practice with number lines and squares can be very helpful.
  Visual counting patterns on a number line can help children to understand relative numbers and number sequences

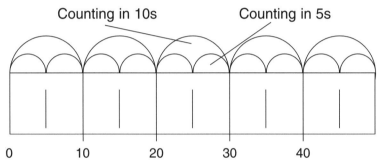

Figure 8.4 Patterns on a number line

They can also provide a visual representation of number operations, e.g:

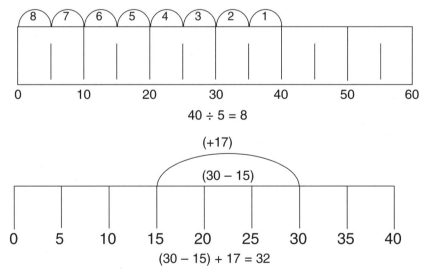

Figure 8.5 Visual representations of number operation

Number lines and number squares are a good way to practise and overlearn the number bonds to 20 which children need to be able to remember fluently.

How do I know whether or not a child has understood a mathematical concept?

There are different levels of understanding mathematical concepts. Almost every mathematics idea, except simple arithmetic facts, consists of three components: *Linguistic, conceptual* and *procedural* (Sharma 1997). At the beginning of learning a new concept we emphasise the language component and the understanding of the new vocabulary, e.g. when learning the concepts of bigger and smaller, children play with a variety of toys and concrete apparatus and the words '*big*' and '*small*' are repeated and emphasised. The use of language helps the understanding of the concept. Without the use of language it would be very hard to teach the concepts of big and small by just looking and feeling big and small objects.

The procedural component comes later on with more formal mathematics operations, when we try to quantify how much bigger or how much smaller.

As children develop understanding of mathematical concepts they go through stages of partial understanding. Initially they can only understand a number concept with the help of apparatus or real objects, e.g. they need to count out real objects. The next stage is to be able to understand the concept with the help of pictures or diagrams:

△
△△ and △△ is △△△△
          △△   △△△

Then they can understand a concept in words and translate them into symbols which is what we do when we write down sums.
3 + 4 = 7
The next stage is to be able to apply that knowledge to a real life situation or problem, e.g. *There are 7 children in the group but only 4 pencils in the pot. How many more pencils are needed?*

The level of complete mastery is achieved when a child (or adult) can explain how they worked out a problem and can teach someone else to do it.

- The higher the level of mastery of a concept the better we are able to remember it. Many adults can work out basic arithmetic sums, e.g. 50 per cent of £200 but have difficulty applying the concepts in more complex real life problems such as working out the amount of interest you will pay on a loan. Many adults will have forgotten much of the maths taught to them at school because they only learned it to the symbolic level, e.g. they can work out a sum but cannot apply that knowledge to real life problems or explain how to work out a problem and why.
- You can check how well a child has understood what they have done by asking them to explain how they solved the problem or get them to try to teach someone else how to do the problem.

Chapter 9

Giving support in the daily maths lesson

The National Numeracy Strategy Framework for teaching mathematics (DfEE 1999b) was published in March 1999. It is intended to complement the National Literacy Strategy and the framework contains a set of yearly mathematics teaching programmes for the time from Reception Year to Year 6 and was introduced into schools from September 1999.

The teaching approach recommended by the National Numeracy Strategy is based on four main principles:

- dedicated mathematics lesson every day;
- direct teaching and interactive oral work with the whole class and groups;
- an emphasis on mental calculation;
- controlled differentiation, with all pupils engaged in mathematics relating to a common theme.

The daily mathematics lesson in Key Stage 1 should be about 45 minutes long and 50 to 60 minutes long in Key Stage 2.

Teachers are also encouraged to develop the mathematical skills of their pupils in other subjects, e.g. design and technology, science, geography, ICT, etc.

Each daily mathematics lesson is structured as follows:

- *oral work and mental calculation*: 5 – 10 minutes.

This session is a combination of teacher input and pupil activities with the class working as a whole, in groups, pairs or individually.

- *main teaching activity*: 30 – 40 minutes.

This part of the lesson is a combination of teacher input and pupil activities with the class working as a whole, in groups or individually

- *plenary session*: 10 – 15 minutes.

What is a typical mathematics lesson?

This session allows the teacher to repeat the main teaching point of the lesson, to summarise the key facts or concepts and to make links with other subjects. It is a time to sort out any problems and assess what progress has been made. It can also be a time when homework is set.

What are oral work and mental calculation?

These take place in the first part of the lesson. The teacher may use this time to practise and improve skills or to focus on a particular skill which will be used in the main part of the lesson.

The activities in this first part of the lesson may include:

- counting – forwards, backwards in different size steps, e.g. counting in 2s, 5s, 10s, etc. – counting on and counting backwards from different numbers;
- practising – mental 'sums' or calculations;
- rehearsing rapid recall of number facts;
- reviewing – teaching points or facts from a previous lesson.

The teacher is likely to ask different pupils questions at a brisk pace and will vary the questions according to the needs and skills of individual pupils.

Teachers will use a variety of *'open'* and *'closed'* questions to help students to respond to the best level of their ability. A closed question is a question that has only one correct answer, e.g. Is 15 a multiple of 5? An *open* question can have several correct answers and allows pupils to show a wider range of skills, e.g. 'Give me a multiple of 5 between 15 and 50'.

Although this session is called a mental maths session, the teacher will encourage the children to use a variety of apparatus to help make sure that all the children can participate fully.

Number cards and number fans help to ensure that all the children respond to the questions not just the quickest and brightest. The use of number cards or fans enables the teacher to quickly see which children have understood a concept or know certain facts.

How will I be able to help children in the mental and oral maths session?

The mental maths session is a whole class teaching session

- Some children who find it hard to focus their attention or who can only concentrate for short periods may need you to prompt them and to instruct them to refocus their attention.
- Although the emphasis in this session is on fluent oral responses and mental calculations it does not mean that concrete apparatus cannot be used.
- Pupils who find learning difficult will be able to respond better if they have a number square or number line in front of them. They may need apparatus such as counters or cubes to assist in counting or calculations.

- As an assistant you can help pupils to respond appropriately by joining in and modelling appropriate responses alongside the pupils.
- If a child has a poor auditory memory and cannot hold figures or calculations in his head, be prepared to repeat the question or to rephrase it to enable the child to join in.
- If the teacher is working from a large number line or number square, make sure the children you support have their own personal line or square on which they can count.
- Check that the size of number cards and number fans are appropriate. Dyspraxic pupils or pupils with fine motor skill difficulties may be able to use larger sized cards or thicker cards more easily.

How can I help children learn number facts?

- Children who find learning difficult often find remembering number facts and multiplication tables difficult. They may need extra regular practice sessions to enable them to remember facts and tables. A multi-sensory approach to learning number facts is usually the most effective method of helping to ensure the facts get into long-term (permanent) memory.
- A modified Look, Read, Cover, Write, Check strategy, that was described for learning reading and spelling vocabulary in Chapter 6, can be applied to number facts.

Read the number fact.
Make the number fact with cubes or counters (for addition and subtraction bonds to 10).
Say the number fact.
Cover the number fact.
Say it to yourself.
Write down the number fact.
Check what you have written.

How can I help children to learn multiplication facts?

Learning multiplication tables by heart can be a major problem for some children, but quick access to these facts is necessary for developing maths skills.

Learning can be assisted in a number of different ways.

- Dictate multiplication tables into a tape recorder, then play it back and write it down to dictation and then check it.
- Learning multiplication tables to a rhythm or rap can help memorisation.
- If memorising number facts and multiplication tables proves to be very difficult then a different approach needs to be taken to make the number facts or tables readily available so they can be referred to quickly when needed.

- A multiplication square or a card with unknown multiplication facts written on it can be very helpful for pupils who cannot remember multiplication tables.
- Some pupils get 'lost' when reciting multiplication tables. They may find it helpful to keep a tally on their fingers as they recite the table.
- Some multiplication tables are easier to learn than others. So a suggested order in which to try to learn them is:
  1 x : 2 x : 10 x : 5 x : 9 x : 3 x : 7 x :
  The 4 x and 8 x tables can be worked out by doubling the 2 x table
  e.g. **2 x 4** : – 2 x 2 = 4
  4 x 2 = **8**
  5 x 8 : – 5 x 2 = 10
  10 x 2 = 20
  20 x 2 = **40**
  The 6 x table can be worked out by doubling the 3 x table
  e.g. **7 x 6** : – 7 x 3 = 21
  21 x 2 = 42
  The 9 x table can be worked out by the finger method (Figures 9.1 and 9.2). Number the fingers (including thumbs) from left to right. Then if the question is "what is 3 x 9?", bend finger number 3. Count the fingers to the left of finger number 3 = 2 – this represents the number of tens.
  Then count the fingers to the right of finger number 3 = 7 – this represents the number of units. The answer is 2 (tens) 7 (units) = 27.

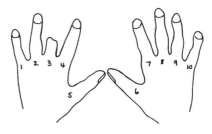

Figure 9.1

For the question, 'what is 7 x 9?', bend finger number 7. The answer is 6 (tens) 3 (units) = 63.

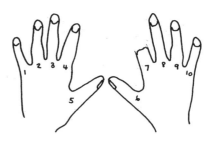

Figure 9.2

- Illustrating multiplication facts using squared paper can help pupils understand what multiplication is, to remember the facts and to estimate the answers.

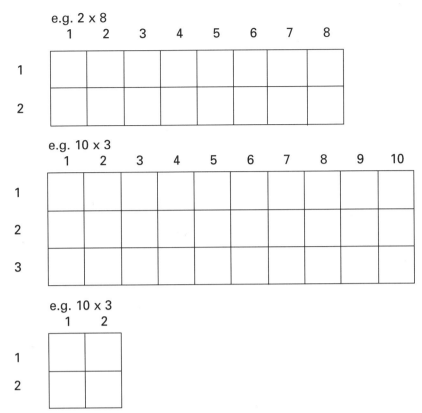

Figure 9.3 Multiplication facts on squared paper

- Older students can become discouraged at their inability to learn and retain multiplication facts. They need to be encouraged to look at how many facts they know and how many more they need to learn.
  (It is important for them to understand reciprocal numbers, that is 6 x 4 is the same as 4 x 6 etc)
  Use a multiplication square to record the number of facts that are known.
- If a pupil can learn the 1x; 2x; 5x; 10x and 9x tables then there are only 8 more multiplication facts to learn:

| 3 x 3 | 7 x 3 | 7 x 4 | 7 x 6 |
| 6 x 3 | 6 x 4 | 6 x 6 | 7 x 7 |

How can I support pupils in the main teaching activity of a daily maths lesson?

- You need to plan and discuss with the teacher before the lesson what the main teaching points and activities of the lesson will be.
- It is the teacher's responsibility to plan the differentiation needed for the pupils who find learning more difficult. As an assistant you will be able to help the teacher by suggesting activities. Feed back to the teacher information about how the children you support coped in the previous lesson and whether they had any significant successes or difficulties.
- You will probably be working with a small group of pupils or an individual pupil. Remember that most pupils who find learning

85

mathematics difficult are likely to be at the concrete or pictorial stage of understanding a concept. They will need lots of practice using concrete apparatus, pictures and diagrams before they will understand written 'sums' completely.

Playing games helps to make the regular overlearning that these pupils will need more interesting and fun. Always try to make activities fun and enjoyable.

- When playing games with children, try to focus on the particular learning target that the game is reinforcing.
- Repeat the teaching instructions given to the pupils by the teacher at the beginning of the session to remind the children of what it is they are trying to learn. You may need to do this several times.
- The teacher is likely to suggest what apparatus or activities to use in supporting the children, but if you find that an individual or group is struggling with an activity do not be afraid to suggest the use of concrete resources.
- Children learn better when they have not only seen and heard information, but have had the opportunity to do it for themselves. They should have the practical experience of weighing and measuring, but may need help in reading the scale of a ruler or tape measure and may get confused by the names of the units of measurement, e.g. millimetres, centimetres, grammes, kilograms, etc.
- In practical activities such as weighing, try not to take over, but guide and support using verbal instructions and be prepared to help clear up the mess at the end!
- Encourage pupils to talk about what they are doing and to reflect on what worked well and what did not. Ask the children to try to explain what they did and why they did it. Remember, the highest level of understanding anything comes when you can explain what you did and teach someone else to do it.
- Getting pupils to 'teach each other' is an excellent way of improving their use of language and their understanding of a new concept. If they get stuck, gently prompt with questions such as 'What did you do next?' 'How did you find that out?' etc.
- The Numeracy Strategy emphasises that there is not just one way to solve a problem or sum. Be sure to praise children for finding different ways of working out problems, always encourage them to reflect on how they solved the problem.
- Some children may have difficulty discriminating the difference between the symbols:
  + and x
  + and ÷
  − and ÷

with consequent confusion and wrong answers. Focus the child's attention at the beginning of the activity. Encourage the child to read all the signs carefully and check which operations will be required in a set of sums.

Highlighting each of the signs +, −, x, and, ÷ first in a different colour, can help focus attention and encourage pupils to look carefully.

The most useful resources are those that are simple, can be adapted to a variety of teaching activities and are fun. As we discussed when we considered resources for literacy, there are hundreds of commercially produced resources.

- Number cards and number fans help to involve all pupils in the oral and mental maths sessions. They can be adapted to be larger or smaller and on different thickness of laminated card for pupils with poor fine motor skills. The numbers can be textured to become tactile to help in developing number writing skills and for visually impaired pupils.
- Number lines are very versatile. They can be any size, for individual or whole-class use. They can start on any number. Blank number lines are infinitely adaptable, they can be used for counting calculations using all four number operations, as in Figure 9.4.

e.g. 50 + 10 + 17 = 77

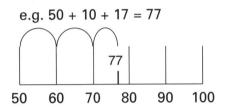

81 ÷ 10 = 8 r 1

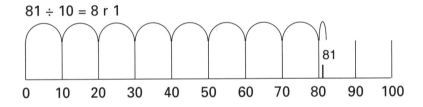

7 x 6 = 42

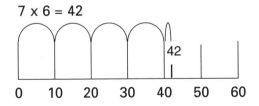

21 − 13 = 8

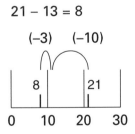

Figure 9.4 Using number lines for all four number options

Blank number lines can be used for:

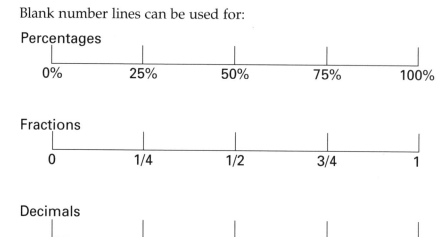

Figure 9.5 Number lines for percentages, fractions and decimals

- When using number lines or number squares, encourage the children to close their eyes and to try to visualise where a number is situated. (This helps with remembering the relative position of numbers in a sequence.)
  Number squares can be used for counting, multiplication tables and demonstrating sequential patterns in numbers. They are often easier to use than a long number line.

Dice

Dice can be used to develop fast number recognition and to move from recognition of numbers by counting to the more abstract ability of instant number recognition. Two or more dice can be used to promote any of the four operations, addition, subtraction, multiplication and division. Dice are available in various 3D shapes with different numbers of faces.

Different types of dominoes are manufactured to help support lots of different mathematical concepts, from simple number dot patterns to various number facts. Again, they are an interesting way for children to practise number recognition skills and to practise number facts. They can be played individually or in a group.

How can I support children during the plenary session?

- Try to plan with the teacher before the lesson the learning outcomes that the teacher expects for the children you are supporting.
- You may need to prepare the child or group for the plenary session so that they are able to report back what they have done and what they have found out.
- Pupils with language or concentration difficulties may need supportive prompting to help them report back verbally. This can

be done by prompt questions, e.g. 'We found out which numbers added up to 10. Which numbers did we find?' or, an additional prompt such as 'We found that 2 and . . . What was the number? Yes, 8 make 10'.

- Use prompts for the children by having the appropriate number cards handy or the number facts written down for the children to refer to.
- The plenary session is often used by the teacher as a time to set homework. Make sure the children have the appropriate instructions written down clearly and legibly so that parents can read them and have any equipment and resources they will need.
- Pre-plan with the teacher whether the children will need differentiated homework tasks or will need to take home any additional support materials, e.g. cubes, number squares, etc, in order to complete homework.
- Feed back to the teacher any particular successes or difficulties the children experienced during the lesson.
- Always try to finish a lesson on a positive note by praising each child for his or her efforts. Celebrate the successes of the lesson and remind them of what they could aim to achieve in the next lesson.

Some final comments

The contribution of assistants in supporting the development of children's literacy and numeracy skills is now being recognised as an important part of their role. Evidence from recent surveys has demonstrated that the support of assistants is making a particular impact in the Literacy Hour and the daily maths lesson, particularly when the respective roles of teacher and assistant are planned. In this planning, assistants are frequently given certain tasks to do so they know what *has* to be done. This book has set out to describe more about *how* this might be done, and done effectively.

An understanding of the development which underpins successful learning, particularly in the area of literacy and numeracy, has been described – how children learn to read, write, spell and understand numbers. The importance of early language and concept development has been explained to enable assistants to have a better understanding of the processes which are fundamental to learning these basic skills.

Practical guidance has been given in the hope that assistants themselves will become effective learners about the children they work with and that they will learn to question the methods they are using, whether the task is at the right level and whether the conditions are right for the child to make progress towards becoming an independent learner.

We hope that this guide will be used by head teachers, teachers and SENCOs to support the assistants they work with. We hope that assistants will use this book to learn new skills in giving support. We hope too that assistants will feel more confident in working with teachers and helping the children to be successful in developing these important basic skills.

Appendix A: Glossary

active voice
the subject of the verb carries out the action, e.g. The boy dropped the ball.

adjective
a word used to describe a noun or pronoun e.g. the *blue* book.

alliteration
the repetition of the initial sound in a sequence of words
e.g.   the silver stars
        the sausages sizzled slowly in the pan.

analogue
clocks and watches that show the time using hands to indicate hours and minutes.

assonance
the repetition of vowel sounds, e.g. sky light, rhyme time.

attention deficit disorder
with or without hyperactivity. Often abbreviated to ADD or ADHD. Typically, individuals cannot remain on task for more than a few minutes. (Those with hyperactivity fidget and appear restless.) They are easily distracted by external stimuli. Socially, they may appear naive, lacking inhibitions or behave inappropriately.

auditory perception
the identification and analysis of information through the ears. There are various elements including:
attention – the ability to focus on or respond to sounds
blending – the ability to blend speech sounds (phonemes) to form words
discrimination – the ability to distinguish between different sounds and noises
localisation – the ability to locate the direction or source of a sound
memory – the ability to store auditory information in short-term memory
sequencing – to be able to recall information in the correct order.

bar chart

a way of displaying information about the number or size of things, e.g. number of children with different types of pets; number of people using different forms of transport.

blend

the ability to combine or blend phonemes into larger sound chunks, e.g. digraphs, trigraphs, syllables and words.

capacity

usually refers to a container and the amount of space inside it.

cloze procedure

words, or phrases are left out of a text. The child has to read or write in a suitable word or phrase.

cognitive

generally used to describe intellectual activity, the thinking or knowing part of an activity rather than feeling.

compound word

a word made up of two words, e.g. carpet, football, supermarket.

comprehension

the understanding of what is said or what is read. In reading there are different levels of comprehension:

– *literal*   the reader can recall the details or events in a text;

– *inferential* the reader can extract information from a text by the use of other information, e.g. if the text describes the weather as frosty, it can be inferred that it is winter time;

– *evaluative* the reader gives an opinion of the quality of the text.

concept

an idea that can be abstract or concrete. Concepts are usually learned through experience or activities and then a verbal label is learned by association, e.g. a young child learns the concept of cold by experiencing cold in relation to ice cream, the fridge, ice cubes, metal objects, etc.

consonant

all the letters of the alphabet are consonants except for a e i o u.

coordination

– the combination of several actions or functions to perform a task;

– gross motor coordination refers to the coordination of muscle activities to perform big movements, e.g. running, walking, sitting;

– fine motor coordination refers to the coordination of small muscle movements to perform precise tasks, e.g. writing, using scissors, picking up small objects;

– hand-eye coordination (also known as visual-motor coordination) is the ability to coordinate visual activities and muscle movements to complete an activity such as hitting a tennis ball with a racquet.

correspondence

matching two separate bits of information, e.g. grapheme – phoneme correspondence is to match letter shapes with the letter sound.

cue
a range of cues, including contextual, grammatical, graphic and phonological are used to decode unfamiliar words.

decode
to convert a written or spoken code into meaningful language.

difference
the difference between two numbers is how much bigger one is than another. The difference is calculated by subtracting the smaller number from the larger number.

digraph
two letters that represent one sound (phoneme) e.g. th – ee – aw.

discrimination
the ability to perceive differences between two or more stimuli.

dyslexia
is a specific learning difficulty usually affecting the ability to read and spell. Now thought to be a genetic neuronal deficiency often affecting auditory memory.

dyspraxia
children with dyspraxia can appear awkward, clumsy and may seem to be slow to respond. There is poor integration of the senses and poor spatial organisation and motor function.

factor
the factors of a number are the smaller numbers that the number can be divided into, e.g. the factors of 20 are 4 and 5 also 2 and 10.

grapheme
one or more letters that represent a simple sound (phoneme).

homonym
two words with the same spelling and sound but different meaning, e.g. fair (pale) fair (impartial).

homophone
two words with the same sound but different spelling, e.g. meat and meet, stare and stair.

kinaesthetic
sensation through which we perceive movement and touch.

medial vowel
the middle vowel in a three letter word, e.g. 'o' in dog, 'u' in cup.

metacognition
an understanding of the learning process and how it develops.

mnemonic
a strategy used to help remember correct spelling. It involves the construction of a sentence with initial letter of each word matching the sequence of letters in the word to be learned.

morpheme
the smallest meaningful unit of a word, e.g. un – re – im – able – re – gain.

multiple
if you multiply one number by another number the answer is a multiple e.g. 6 x 2 = 12, the multiple is 12 – 6, 12, 18, 24, 30 are all multiples of 6.

multi-sensory
  using all the sensory pathways, kinaesthetic, visual, auditory.
negative numbers
  numbers less than zero, e.g. – 5 – 4 – 3 – 2 – 1.
net
  a net is the pattern or shape you get when you unfold a three dimensional shape, e.g. if you unfold and flatten a box.
number bonds
  also known as number facts. Children need to be able to remember basic number facts fluently.
onset
  as in 'onset and rhyme'. The onset may be an initial consonant, consonant blend or digraph.
operations
  refers to the four main operations of number:
  + addition: – subtraction: x multiplication: ÷ division.
paired reading
  a way of sharing a book with a child in which the adult and child read aloud together.
phoneme
  the smallest unit of speech, it may be represented by one or more letters.
phonetics
  the study of speech sounds.
phonics
  a strategy for decoding words by linking sounds (phonemes) to letter symbols (graphemes).
phonological awareness
  awareness of sounds and being able to recognise and manipulate sounds.
place value
  when we write numbers above 9, the position in the sequence indicates the value of each number, e.g. 42 – four is worth 40
  two is worth 2.
plenary
  the plenary comes at the end of a literacy hour or a maths lesson. It is the time for the teacher to revise the teaching targets of the lesson and to assess the learning outcomes and what the children have learned. It is also a time for the children to reflect on what they have done and how well they have achieved the targets.
product
  when two numbers are multiplied together the answer is called the product e.g. the product of 5 x 2 is 10.
quotient
  the answer to a division sum, e.g. 60 ÷ 10 the quotient is 6.
reading age
  an individual's performance on a standardised reading test expressed as the reading standard for the average child in a specific age group.

rhyme
> words containing the same rime in the final syllable.
> e.g. dig, pig; grow, slow

rime
> the part of a syllable which contains the vowel and the final consonant or consonant cluster, if there is one; e.g. – at in cat; – orn in horn; – ow in cow. Some words consist of rime only, e.g. or, ate, owl (DfEE 1998a).

scan
> to look over a text very quickly usually to find a key word or specific information; to analyse the rhythm of a line of poetry.

segment
> to break words into their component phonemes, e.g. man – m – a – n or into syllables, e.g. letter – let – ter.

semantic cue
> information from meaning of words, phrases or sentences, used to help in the identification of an unfamiliar word.

shared reading
> a strategy used by the teacher where the teacher models reading skills with a group of children.

shared writing
> a teaching strategy where the teacher demonstrates and models writing skills for a group of children.

sight vocabulary
> words which a child can read automatically as whole words.

skimming
> a method of rapid reading to gain the main idea of a text.

spatial orientation
> awareness of how the body relates to the environment or how shapes and objects relate to each other in space.

visual discrimination
> the ability to perceive similarities and differences in visually presented material.

visual memory
> the ability to store visually presented information in order to analyse it and recall it accurately.

visual perception
> the organisation and interpretation of information received through the eyes.

visual sequencing
> the order in which visual information is presented.

vowel
> the vowel letters are a e i o u – every syllable in a word must contain a vowel.

writing frame
> any structure that supports writing. It may consist of pictures, diagrams, headings or questions. It may be in the form of a template for a specific writing format.

Appendix B: Vocabulary lists

High frequency words to be taught as 'sight recognition' words through YR to Y2. Taken from The National Literacy Strategy Framework for teaching literacy (DfEE 1998).

Reception Year

I	go	come	went
up	you	day	was
look	are	the	of
we	this	dog	me
like	going	big	she
and	they	my	see
on	away	mum	it
at	play	no	yes
for	a	dad	can
he	am	all	
is	cat	get	
said	to	in	

Years 1 to 2

about	brother	first
after	but	from
again	by	girl
an	call(ed)	good
another	came	got
as	can't	had
back	could	half
ball	did	has
be	dig	have
because	do	help
bed	don't	her
been	door	here
boy	down	him

Years 1 to 2

his
home
house
how
if
jump
just
last
laugh
little
live(d)
love
made
make
man
many
may
more
much
must
name
new
next
night
not
now
off

pld
once
one
or
our
out
over
people
push
pull
put
ran
saw
school
seen
should
sister
so
some
take
than
that
their
them
then
there
these

three
time
too
took
tree
two
us
very
want
water
way
were
what
when
where
who
will
with
would
your

Plus:
• days of the week;
• months of the year;
• numbers to twenty;
• common colour words;
• pupil's name and address;
• name and address of school

List 2

High frequency words to be taught through Year 4 and 5

above
across
almost
along
also
always
animals
any
around
asked
baby
balloon
before
began
being
below
better
between
birthday

both
brother
brought
can't
change
children
clothes
coming
didn't
different
does
don't
during
earth
every
eyes
father
first
follow(ing)

found
friends
garden
goes
gone
great
half
happy
head
heard
high
I'm
important
inside
jumped
knew
know
lady
leave

List 2 (cont.)

light	sister	under
might	small	until
money	something	upon
morning	sometimes	used
mother	sound	walk(ed)(ing)
much	started	watch
near	still	where
never	stopped	while
number	such	white
often	suddenly	whole
only	sure	why
opened	swimming	window
other	think	without
outside	those	woke(n)
own	thought	word
paper	through	work
place	today	world
right	together	write
round	told	year
second	tries	young
show	turn(ed)	

Resources

Language Master system available from:

Drake Educational Associates, St. Fagans Road, Fairwater, Cardiff CF5 3AE

ACE Spelling Dictionary – David Moseley – Published by LDA

Appendix C: Early Learning Goals

The objectives set out in the National Literacy Strategy: *Framework for Teaching* for the reception year are in line with these goals. By the end of the foundation stage, most children will be able to:

- enjoy listening to and using spoken and written language, and readily turn to it in their play and learning;
- explore and experiment with sounds, words and texts;
- listen with enjoyment and respond to stories, songs and other music, rhymes and poems and make up their own stories, songs, rhymes and poems;
- use language to imagine and recreate roles and experiences;
- use talk to organise, sequence and clarify thinking, ideas, feelings and events;
- sustain attentive listening, responding to what they have heard by relevant comments, questions and actions;
- interact with others, negotiating plans and activities and taking turns in conversation;
- extend their vocabulary, exploring the meanings and sounds of new words;
- retell narratives in the correct sequence, drawing on the language patterns of stories;
- speak clearly and audibly with confidence and control and show awareness of the listener, for example by their use of conventions such as greetings, 'please' and 'thank you';
- hear and say initial and final sounds in words, and short vowel sounds within words;
- link sounds to letters, naming and sounding the letters of the alphabet;
- read a range of familiar and common words and simple sentences independently;
- know that print carries meaning and, in English, is read from left to right and top to bottom;
- show an understanding of the elements of stories, such as main character, sequence of events, and openings, and how information

Early learning goals for language and literacy

can be found in non-fiction texts to answer questions about where, who, why and how;

- attempt writing for various purposes, using features of different forms such as lists, stories and instructions;
- write their own names and other things such as labels and captions and begin to form simple sentences, sometimes using punctuation;
- use their phonic knowledge to write simple regular words and make phonetically plausible attempts at more complex words;
- use a pencil and hold it effectively to form recognisable letters, most of which are correctly formed.

Early learning goals for mathematical development

The key objectives in the National Numeracy Strategy: *Framework for Teaching* for the reception year are in line with these goals. By the end of the foundation stage, most children will be able to:

- say and use number names in order in familiar contexts;
- count reliably up to 10 everyday objects;
- recognise numerals 1 to 9;
- use language, such as 'more' or 'less', 'greater' or 'smaller', 'heavier' or 'lighter', to compare two numbers or quantities;
- in practical activities and discussion begin to use the vocabulary involved in adding and subtracting;
- find one more or one less than a number from 1 to 10;
- begin to relate addition to combining two groups of objects, and subtraction to 'taking away';
- talk about, recognise and recreate simple patterns;
- use language such as 'circle' or 'bigger' to describe the shape and size of solids and flat shapes;
- use everyday words to describe position;
- use developing mathematical ideas and methods to solve practical problems.

Bibliography

Ainscow, M. and Tweddle, D. A. (1988) *Encouraging Classroom Success.* London: David Fulton Publishers.

Aplin, Ruth (1998) *Assisting Numeracy – A Handbook for Classroom Assistants.* London: Beam Education Limited.

Audit Commission/HMI (1992) *Getting in on the Act: A Management Handbook for Schools and LEAs.* London: HMSO.

Barrs, K. and Logan, S. (1998) *A Number of Things.* Dunstable: Belair Publications (Folen).

Basic Skills Agency (1997) *Basic Skills Support in School: A Guide for Every Teacher.* (Basic Skills Agency)

Beam Mathematics (1998) *Literacy and Numeracy Project.* London: Beam Mathematics.

Brooks, P. and Weeks, S. (1999) *Individual Styles in Learning to Spell: Improving Spelling in Children with Literacy Difficulties and all Children in Mainstream Schools.* Research Report RR108. Nottingham: DfEE.

Chinn, S. and Ashcroft, M. (1998) *Mathematics for Dyslexics. A Teaching Handbook*, 2nd edn. London: Whurr.

DfEE (1997) *Excellence for All Children: Meeting Special Educational Needs.* (Green Paper). London: HMSO.

DfEE (1998a) The National Literacy Strategy. *A Framework for Teaching Literacy.* London: HMSO.

DfEE (1998b) *Teachers Meeting the Challenge of Change.* (Green Paper). London: HMSO.

DfEE (1999a) Additional Literacy Support (Module 1) (National Literacy Strategy). London: HMSO.

DfEE (1999b) National Numeracy Strategy. *A Framework for Teaching Mathematics.* London: HMSO.

DfEE (1999c) *Early Learning Goals.* London: HMSO.

Hampshire Inspection and Advisory Support Service, Hampshire Education Authority (1992) *Principles of Good Practice. A Tool for Self-evaluation.* Hampshire LEA.

Henderson, A. (1989) *Maths and Dyslexics.* Llandudno: St. David's College.

Henderson, A. (1998) *Maths for the Dyslexic. A Practical Guide.* London: David Fulton Publishers.

Jager-Adams, M. (1990) *Beginning to Read: The New Phonics in Context.* London: Heinemann).

Moseley, D. and Nichol, K. (1986) *Aurally Coded English (ACE) Spelling Dictionary.* London: LDA.

Poole, Borough of, 'Scaffolding Activities Focusing on Literacy Difficulties' (unpublished).

Sharma, M. C. (1981) 'Prerequisite and Support Skills for Mathematics Learning'. *Math Notebook* **2**(1). Mass, USA. Center for Teaching/Learning Mathematics.

Sharma, M. C. (1990) 'Concept of Number'. *Math Notebook* **8**(1, 2). Mass, USA. Center for Teaching/Learning Mathematics.

Sharma, M. C. (1997) Diagnostic and Remedial Perspectives in Mathematics: Factors affecting Mathematics Learning. Unpublished notes.

QCA (1999) *Standards in Mathematics: Exemplifications of Key Learning Objectives.* London: Qualifications and Curriculum Authority.

University of Manchester and DfEE (1999) *The Management Role and Training of Learning Support Assistants.* A research report for the DfEE.

University of Warwick, Essex LEA and the Leverhulme Trust (December 1998) *Early Reading Research. Summary and Results.*

Index